Using Authentic Assessment in Information Literacy Programs

Using Authentic Assessment in Information Literacy Programs

Tools, Techniques, and Strategies

Jennifer S. Ferguson

ROWMAN & LITTLEFIELD
Lanham • Boulder • New York • London

3780 BP53

Published by Rowman & Littlefield
An imprint of The Rowman & Littlefield Publishing Group, Inc.
4501 Forbes Boulevard, Suite 200, Lanham, Maryland 20706
www.rowman.com

Unit A, Whitacre Mews, 26-34 Stannary Street, London SE11 4AB

British Library Cataloguing in Publication Information Available

Library of Congress Cataloging-in-Publication Data Available

ISBN 9781538104804 (hardback : alk. paper) | ISBN 9781538104811 (pbk. : alk. paper) | ISBN 9781538104828 (electronic)

∞™ The paper used in this publication meets the minimum requirements of American National Standard for Information Sciences—Permanence of Paper for Printed Library Materials, ANSI/NISO Z39.48-1992.

Printed in the United States of America

12|28|20

Contents

Acknowledgments

Many people made this book possible, and I couldn't have conceived of this project without their help, advice, and guidance at many points during the writing process. First, I would like to thank Todd Gilman for seeing something in my work that I didn't necessarily see myself and for making its dissemination to a wider audience possible. My editor, Charles Harmon, also saw merit in this project and made the writing process a pleasure. In addition, my husband, Steven Scherwatzky, offered the help, encouragement, and confidence that I needed to write this book. His support and understanding made everything easier. I continue to be grateful to Shanti Freundlich and Jeremy Shaw-Munderback, my friends and former colleagues at Beatley Library, Simmons College, for the many insights I gained from our conversations over the years. Lastly, it is important for me to acknowledge all of the great faculty members that I worked with at Simmons College, especially Kelly Hager, Margaret Hanni, and Renee Bergland, who allowed me to test many of the methods described in this book with their classes and who provided invaluable feedback along the way.

List of Tables, Figures, and Sample Forms

CHAPTER 2

CHAPTER 4

CHAPTER 5

CHAPTER 6

Preface

Driven by state and federal guidelines, accrediting agencies, and consumer demand, assessment of student learning outcomes and objectives is a significant ongoing topic in higher education. For academic librarians who provide information literacy instruction, creating and implementing authentic assessment instruments, which require students to analyze, synthesize, and apply what they have learned, is especially challenging since most librarians have little more than an hour in which to teach students and assess their learning.

Using Authentic Assessment in Information Literacy Programs: Tools, Techniques, and Strategies is meant to provide academic librarians with a starting point for understanding the basics of authentic assessment within the context of information literacy instruction. It is intended to help clarify the meaning of assessment and differentiate between modes of assessment, allowing academic librarians to choose the techniques that work best within their instructional settings. *Using Authentic Assessment in Information Literacy Programs: Tools, Techniques, and Strategies* is the first book to provide an in-depth look at the state of authentic assessment in academic libraries, offer guidelines for implementation, and connect it to the Association of College and Research Libraries' Framework for Information Literacy for Higher Education (the ACRL framework). In addition, this book delves into the origin of authentic assessment, defines it across a variety of educational settings, explains how theory has been translated into practice, and also highlights exemplary case studies that demonstrate how authentic assessment is being used in academic libraries today.

Each chapter addresses key aspects of authentic assessment. As a whole, the book offers an in-depth look at specific issues in authentic assessment, including how it has been discussed by educators at every level, from its origins in the late 1980s to the present, through the current status of authentic assessment in academic libraries.

Chapter 1 examines the literature on authentic assessment, explains its theoretical underpinnings, and defines it within the larger educational context, while chapter 2 highlights the literature reflecting the current state of authentic assessment in academic libraries both in the United States and internationally. Chapter 3 describes the advantages and challenges of the most common authentic assessment instruments outlined in the literature; chapter 4 uses case studies to highlight how academic librarians have employed those instruments in practice. Chapter 5 highlights case studies across instructional contexts, demonstrating how authentic assessment techniques have been adapted to the most common types of instruction—from credit-bearing courses, to embedded librarianship, online instruction, and one-shot sessions. Chapter 6 provides step-by-step guidelines for designing instruction sessions to incorporate authentic teaching and assessment, including sample assessment instruments. Finally, chapter 7 addresses future directions in authentic assessment, drawing once again on literature that focuses on a wide array of educational settings, including academic libraries, while chapter 8 connects authentic assessment to the ACRL framework, stakeholder requirements, and more.

Using Authentic Assessment in Information Literacy Programs: Tools, Techniques, and Strategies will help academic librarians understand what is meant by the term authentic assessment and how it differs from more common forms of assessment. In addition, each chapter will help teaching librarians to synthesize the literature on authentic assessment, analyze the strengths and weaknesses of authentic assessment instruments within common instructional contexts, select an appropriate mode of assessment for their library, and adapt authentic assessment for their classrooms. Getting started with assessment—especially authentic assessment—can appear to be an overwhelming challenge, and this book is intended to demystify authentic assessment by defining the terminology, describing how it is used in practice, and providing a practical roadmap for implementation.

1

Authentic Assessment Defined

What are we talking about when we talk about "authentic" assessment? Assessment in all its many forms is a topic that academic librarians discuss and debate endlessly across a variety of contexts. We ask ourselves what we need to measure and then try to determine how to measure it. We also ask ourselves whether or not what we're measuring actually tells us anything useful. For example, do circulation statistics tell us anything about what a student thought about the material checked out? Do the number of reference transactions tell us anything about the quality of the interaction or the satisfaction of the patron? Does the raw gate count tell us anything about who visited the library and why? Similarly, does the total number of information literacy instruction sessions tell us anything about what students learned in class?

These kinds of questions have led academic librarians to reconsider what it is that we're trying to assess and what types of questions we should ask in order to get the answers we need, not only to demonstrate value but also to improve our practice. This process is especially acute within the context of information literacy instruction, where more often than not librarians get "one shot" in which to teach incoming first-year students everything they need to know about finding, evaluating, and using information sources. However, it can be difficult to measure anything useful about learning, as opposed to teaching, during a one-shot session. Generally, the assessments that we implement—from short formative measures to online surveys—tell us more about the students' satisfaction, or dissatisfaction, with the library instruction session itself rather than anything about what they actually learned from it.

Over the years, instruction librarians have implemented a wide variety of assessment instruments, with the intention of measuring something useful, or at least something worth knowing, about how students experience library instruction. But within the parameters in which instruction librarians work, learning anything useful can be quite a challenge. From surveys that measure more about how a student feels about the temperature of the room or the time of day to minute papers that may, perhaps, tell us a little bit about what a student found confusing at a given moment or as explained by a particular instructor, the assessment instruments implemented by most librarians in most academic libraries tell us very little about the actual learning that takes place during an information literacy instruction session. This situation is especially critical within the current environment of information overload and so-called fake news. If librarians are tasked with teaching students how to navigate not only the library's resources but also the vast terrain of the web, in about an hour, in, typically, a first-year class, the challenges for instructional design alone are massive. Throw in assessment, and librarians often throw their hands up.

But what if librarians can employ "authentic assessment" instruments within that admittedly difficult context? And what is "authentic assessment," anyway? The first step to understanding and implementing authentic assessment is for librarians to explore theories of teaching and learning outside of the academic library. Educators in other disciplines often develop practices that can be adapted to library instruction. However, there have been many traditional barriers to librarians learning from or collaborating with discipline-specific instructors. This situation is replicated across a variety of library settings, including public, school, and academic libraries (Latham et al. 2016), which makes cross-disciplinary learning challenging. In addition, many researchers have found that "the status of librarians on campus is a barrier to the development of collaborative teaching partnerships between academics and librarians" (Ivey 2003), which can also inhibit the adoption of teaching, learning, and assessment strategies that originate in other areas. Along with that issue, as Ruth Ivey notes, librarians' lack of knowledge about learning theory can present a barrier not only to effective teaching but also to effective evaluation. In addition, librarians "often perceive faculty to be reticent in working with them," with faculty members sometimes "doubtful of librarians' preparation to be teachers" (Saunders 2012).

This anxiety can lead teaching librarians to become insular in their practices, resist the Association of College and Research Libraries (ACRL) Framework for Information Literacy (ACRL 2015), and fail to address the rapidly evolving needs of today's college students. As noted by Dorothy Mays, in order to address these needs we need to turn "away from the reliance on tried-and-true periodical databases" so that our students can "delve into the wider world of information, which will be an excellent vehicle for addressing the new framework" (Mays 2016). These challenges can become even more pronounced when academic librarians attempt to assess student learning. While alternative pedagogies can be adapted somewhat readily to information literacy instruction, adopting more authentic assessment techniques can be much more difficult. Authentic assessment instruments "often ask students to analyze, synthesize and apply what they have learned in a substantial manner" (Mueller 2016), which can be especially demanding for librarians who have an hour not only to teach students what they need to know but also to determine whether or not students actually learned anything.

To begin, we need to understand how authentic assessment is defined and implemented across disciplines and within a variety of learning environments. In addition, librarians should recognize and find comfort in the notion that "many instructors in tertiary education have yet to implement authentic assessment" themselves, for a variety of reasons, including "lack of knowledge of teaching methods and learning principles" (Litchfield and Dempsey 2015). Even when faculty are comfortable with these teaching methods and learning principles, there has still been concern that "performance assessments aren't always practical in terms of time, space, effort and supervision required for successful completion especially when classes are large," prompting Barbara Yunker to propose a hybrid model in which "a multiple choice test can become a useful vehicle for authentic, performance-based assessment" (Yunker 1999). Indeed, considering that authentic assessments ask that "students perform a task rather than select answers" and that those tasks are "related to the topic they are studying, as in general education courses" (Litchfield and Dempsey 2015), this mode of assessment may seem difficult, if not impossible to achieve in the ubiquitous one-shot instruction session. Thus librarians are not necessarily behind the times in implementing authentic assessment but rather are part of a larger trend in higher education, where student needs seem to have outstripped both traditional teaching and modes of assessment.

In 1989, Grant Wiggins advocated for creating more authentic tests, maintaining that teaching to the test would be less of a problem if the tests themselves "were instructional: the central vehicle for clarifying and setting intellectual standards" (Wiggins 1989). That same year, Lorrie A. Shepard argued that educators in primary and secondary schools needed "better assessments," maintaining that "not surprisingly, students given instruction aimed at conceptual understanding do better on skills tests than students drilled on the skills directly." She went on to say, "The best way to check for these indicators is to make assessment measures resemble learning tasks" (Shepard 1989). At the same time, the teacher-designed California Assessment Program (CAP) was developed, with the designers observing that "practical" assessment had already been implemented in England and educators in California planned to "directly measure key process skills—observing, comparing, communicating, organizing, relating, referring, and applying" knowledge (CAP 1989). This discussion in primary and secondary education continued throughout the 1990s. For example, in a paper presented at the Annual Meeting of the American Educational Research Association in 1990, Judith Torney-Purta remarked that "authentic measures are not restricted to recall and do not reflect lucky or unlucky one-shot responses" (Torney-Purta 1990). By the mid-1990s, a number of handbooks and measurement texts had been published that defined authentic assessment as the performance or demonstration of real-life tasks and provided context in order to help teachers understand the concept and learn how to implement it (Hart 1994).

By the late 1990s, authentic assessment was well established in K–12 education. For example, in 1995 Susan Stewart, Joyce Choate, and James Poteet stated, "Alternatives to traditional, standardized assessment have been described by many labels, including direct assessment, performance assessment, authentic assessment, and portfolio assessment," with the common denominator "the type of response required of the student." They went on to say, "Alternative assessment approaches require the student to produce, recall, construct, or demonstrate a response. This demonstration of knowledge closely approximates the way a student will use the information in real life" (Stewart, Choate, and Poteet 1995). The discussion had progressed to the point that, by 1999, the value of authentic assessment was fairly well accepted and authentic assessment instruments were increasingly implemented, leading J. Joy Cumming and Graham S. Maxwell to assert, "The concept of authentic assessment has been embraced enthusiastically by policy makers, curriculum developers and practitioners alike, and enshrined in the literature on curriculum and assessment as a desirable characteristic of education" (Cumming and Maxwell 1999). At that point, the concept was so widely accepted that some researchers began to worry that authentic assessment techniques might do nothing to improve the achievement of diverse students and perhaps might even hamper it, since "low-scoring groups (e.g., English language learners) receive relatively few instructional opportunities to learn skills appearing in performance assessments," though in the end they could provide "an appealing complement to selected-response tests" (Braden 1999).

Over the past ten years, authentic assessment in primary and secondary education has become such an accepted concept that most of the recent literature on the subject focuses on methodologies rather than on arguing for or against it. For example, by September 2016, authentic assessment was described as "a venerable idea," with the current need for "professional strategies" that facilitate "an optimal authentic assessment experience" (Macy, Bagnato, and Gallen 2016). In addition, by early 2017 a search of the ERIC database for "authentic assessment" that limited the results to the past ten years turned up 293 items, with the most common descriptors including evaluation methods, teaching methods, scoring rubrics, and case studies. Interestingly, the higher education descriptor falls just below the top ten (in twelfth place), which demonstrates that while authentic assessment is still not as widely discussed in colleges and universities, it is an ongoing topic of some interest, though, as with most topics in higher education, not without controversy. Along with concerns about how well authentic assessment serves diverse populations, there is also some worry that, with the "growing push to use authentic assessment for accountability in higher education" (Hathcoat et al. 2016), there may be some validity issues based on assignment characteristics and the absence of standardization. In addition, "assessing critical thinking (CT) solely through written products" might prove problematic "since differences in written communication (WC) may act as a source of systematic error" (Hathcoat et al. 2016). However, based on a wide survey of the literature on authentic assessment, Frey, Schmitt, and Allen suggest that "elements of authenticity which will likely increase validity" do not necessarily have to be present in order to consider an assessment technique to be authentic. Instead, as long as a number of "crucial elements" are included in an assessment, such as tasks that involve "the student deeply, both in terms of cognitive complexity and intrinsic interest, and are meant to develop or evaluate skills or abilities that have value beyond the assessment itself" (Frey, Schmitt, and Allen 2012), then it can be considered authentic.

Despite some trepidation, higher education institutions have adopted and implemented authentic assessment in a wide variety of settings, including undergraduate, graduate, and professional education, using a number of different methodologies. These methods include "performance, portfolio, cooperative learning groups, peer teaching, exit cards, journals, exhibitions, demonstrations of understanding, simulations, observations," and many others (Davies and Wavering 1999). While these assessment techniques may seem unrelated, they all embrace a common design that "includes identifying specific and clear criteria for evaluating student performances," with the criteria for evaluation "communicated to students in advance" (Davies and Wavering 1999). In 2006, Herrington and Herrington elaborated on their earlier guidelines for developing authentic assessment instruments and categorized them as "context, student factors, task factors and indicators," maintaining that "such guidelines enable teachers to create learning environments using authentic contexts and scenarios that ensure assessment truly measures whether students can use their knowledge effectively and realistically, as opposed to the reproduction of surface knowledge that is quickly forgotten after an examination or test" (Herrington and Herrington 2006). And because "most students focus more on assessment than any other aspect of their courses," it becomes increasingly important that assessment is used not just as a measurement but also as a learning tool and that educators harness the opportunity it offers to drive student engagement, since "students have a vested interest in passing their course and, therefore, value the importance of this kind of assessment" (Kearney 2013). In a study that compares assessment across disciplines, Tansy Jessop and Barbara Maleckar point out that different assessment techniques can have an impact on student learning, since "authentic assessment motivates students and nurtures deep learning through fostering connections across whole programmes of study, and with wider 'real-world' domains" (Jessop and Maleckar 2016).

This idea of the wider 'real-world' learning implications of authentic assessment becomes especially important as government agencies and accrediting bodies demand accountability and focus on outcomes such as post-graduation employment rates as opposed to more general educational or intellectual attainment. Given this pressure,

> current assessment practices probably constitute insufficient programmatic assessment to satisfy government and accreditation stakeholders, and many programs will be better served by using more standardized assessment measures that demonstrate performance and value-added knowledge. Actual performance, as opposed to academic learning alone, is a major concern at colleges and universities nationally (Hailstorks et al. 2016).

Thus, "a structured, multi-faceted assessment approach" that includes authentic assessments "provides educators with a feasible strategy to demonstrate their effectiveness and impact in meeting learning objectives set forth by accrediting bodies while providing valuable and desired feedback to students" (Misyak et al. 2016). Jion Liou Yen and Kevin Hynes also suggest that, "from a utilitarian assessment perspective, a rubric will have served its purpose well if accreditors . . . or other stakeholders accept the evidentiary argument of valid learning" (Yen and Hynes 2012) that is conveyed by that rubric. In higher education, this combination—demonstrating teaching effectiveness and addressing student learning needs—is driving the move toward authentic assessment. To be considered authentic, an assessment needs to ask students to analyze information, synthesize knowledge, and apply it to a relevant task. In addition, for students to learn from this exercise, they need to be informed of the expectations in advance and be provided with constructive feedback throughout the process. Accomplishing both of these goals simultaneously can be a tremendous challenge in higher education, since each discipline faces its own specific demands in teaching, learning, and assessment (Jessop and Maleckar 2016). Along with those disciplinary demands, Martin Turner and Rachel Baskerville also found that "assessment involving interesting and challenging assessed learning tasks that are individualised, authentic and with regular formative and summative feedback" can help students "to experience deep learning" (Turner and Baskerville 2013). But creating "individualized" learning tasks while promoting deep learning can also be significantly time consuming for faculty, who "may already be overwhelmed by their daily duties of giving classes, researching and publishing, attending meetings, serving on committees, advising students, and so forth" (Bahous and Nabhani 2015).

Despite all of these complications, the need for more authentic assessment in higher education—while slow to be implemented—is understood to be valuable (Litchfield and Dempsey 2015), and most of the current discussion surrounds adapting these techniques to specific subjects, classroom contexts, and student learning needs and then adopting them in a more programmatic fashion. In both K–12 and higher education, there appears to be strong philosophical agreement that assessments "need to resemble learning tasks" and that these learning tasks should closely approximate "the way a student will use the information in real life." In addition, assessment should truly measure "whether students can use their knowledge effectively and realistically." Assessment that is more authentic should also promote deeper learning with real-world problem solving leading students to reflect on their learning and internalize it rather than simply memorizing, regurgitating, and forgetting—since "students who see assessment as closely tied to relevant activities are more likely to engage in learning" (Litchfield and Dempsey 2015).

While this type of assessment can seem daunting, many techniques currently in use have been shown to accomplish the goals of authentic assessment. These methods, among many others, include portfolios, concept mapping, short-answer quizzes, reflections and responses, peer evaluation, and case studies (Mueller 2016). The key to an authentic assessment is to assign a relevant learning task, provide clear performance expectations such as a grading rubric, provide an opportunity for reflection, and offer meaningful feedback in order to foster deep learning. Authentic assessment is not merely about grading; instead, it is about creating a circle in which assigned tasks, student learning, and indicators of success work together. Along with fostering deeper student learning, the real-world implications of this type of teaching and assessment have the potential to demonstrate institutional effectiveness to key stakeholders in a more significant way. Moreover, within the microcosm of individual academic institutions, libraries implementing assessment techniques that more authentically demonstrate their impact on student learning have the potential to overcome some of the well-known barriers to developing collaborative teaching partnerships on campus.

REFERENCES

Association of College and Research Libraries (ACRL). 2015. "Framework for Information Literacy for Higher Education." American Library Association. February 9. http://www.ala.org/acrl/standards/ilframework.

Bahous, Rima, and Mona Nabhani. 2015. "Faculty Views on Developing and Assessing Learning Outcomes at the Tertiary Level." *JGE: Journal of General Education* 64 (4): 294–309.

Braden, Jeffery P. 1999. "Performance Assessment and Diversity." *School Psychology Quarterly* 14, no. 3 (Fall): 304–26.

California Assessment Program (CAP). 1989. "Authentic Assessment in California." *Educational Leadership* 46, no. 7 (April): 6.

Cumming, J. Joy, and Graham S. Maxwell. 1999. "Contextualising Authentic Assessment." *Assessment in Education: Principles, Policies and Practices* 6 (2): 77–194.

Davies, Mary Ann, and Michael Wavering. 1999. "Alternative Assessment: New Directions in Teaching and Learning." *Contemporary Education* 71, no. 1 (Fall): 39–45.

Frey, Bruce B., Vicki L. Schmitt, and Justin P. Allen. 2012. "Defining Authentic Classroom Assessment." *Practical Assessment, Research and Evaluation* 17, no. 2 (January): 1–18.

Hailstorks, Robin, John C. Norcross, Rory A. Pfund, Leona S. Aiken, Karen E. Stamm, and Peggy Christidis. 2016. "Assessment Drivers and Practices in Undergraduate Psychology Programs: A Survey of Associate and Baccalaureate Degree Programs." *Scholarship of Teaching and Learning in Psychology* 2, no. 2 (June): 99111.

Hart, Diane. 1994. *Authentic Assessment: A Handbook for Educators*. Menlo Park, CA: Addison-Wesley.

Hathcoat, John D., Jeremy D. Penn, Laura L. B. Barnes, and Johnathan C. Comer. 2016. "A Second Dystopia in Education: Validity Issues in Authentic Assessment Practices." *Research in Higher Education* 57, no. 7 (November): 892–912.

Herrington, Janice A., and Anthony J. Herrington. 2006. "Authentic Conditions for Authentic Assessment: Aligning Task and Assessment." In *Proceedings of the 2006 Annual International Conference of the Higher Education Research and Development Society of Australasia Inc. (HERDSA): Critical Visions: Thinking, Learning and Researching in Higher Education: Research and Development in Higher Education*, edited by A. Bunker and I. Vardi, 141–51. Milperra, NSW: HERDSA.

Ivey, Ruth. 2003. "Information Literacy: How Do Librarians and Academics Work in Partnership to Deliver Effective Learning Programs?" *Australian Academic and Research Libraries* 34 (2): 100–113.

Jessop, Tansy, and Barbara Maleckar. 2016. "The Influence of Disciplinary Assessment Patterns on Student Learning: A Comparative Study." *Studies in Higher Education* 41 (4): 696–711.

Kearney, Sean. 2013. "Improving Engagement: The Use of 'Authentic Self- and Peer-Assessment for Learning' to Enhance the Student Learning Experience." *Assessment and Evaluation in Higher Education* 38, no. 7 (November): 875–91.

Latham, Don, Heidi Julien, Melissa Gross, and Shelbie Witte. 2016. "The Role of Inter-Professional Collaboration to Support Science Learning: An Exploratory Study of the Perceptions and Experiences of Science Teachers, Public Librarians, and School Librarians." *Library and Information Science Research* 38, no. 3 (July): 193–201.

Litchfield, Brenda C., and John V. Dempsey. 2015. "Authentic Assessment of Knowledge, Skills, and Attitudes." *New Directions for Teaching and Learning* 142 (Summer): 65–80.

Macy, Marisa, Stephen J. Bagnato, and Robert Gallen. 2016. "Authentic Assessment: A Venerable Idea Whose Time Is Now." *Zero to Three* 37, no. 1 (September): 37–43.

Mays, Dorothy A. 2016. "Using ACRL's Framework to Support the Evolving Needs of Today's College Students." *College and Undergraduate Libraries* 23 (4): 353–62.

Misyak, Sarah, Jennifer Culhane, Kathryne McConnell, and Elena Serrano. 2016. "Assessment for Learning: Integration of Assessment in a Nutrition Course with a Service-Learning Component." *NACTA Journal* 60, no. 4 (December): 358–63.

Mueller, Jon. 2016. "What Is Authentic Assessment?" *Authentic Assessment Toolbox,* July 1. http://jfmueller.faculty.noctrl.edu/toolbox/whatisit.htm.

Saunders, Laura. 2012. "Faculty Perspectives on Information Literacy as a Student Learning Outcome." *Journal of Academic Librarianship* 38 (4): 226–36.

Shepard, Lorrie A. 1989. "Why We Need Better Assessments." *Educational Leadership* 46, no. 7 (April): 4–9.

Stewart, Susan C., Joyce S. Choate, and James A. Poteet. 1995. "The Revolution in Assessment within and across Educational Settings." *Preventing School Failure* 39, no. 3 (Spring): 20–24.

Torney-Purta, Judith. 1990. "Measuring Performance in Social Studies in an Authentic Fashion." Presentation at the Annual Meeting of the American Educational Research Association, Boston, April 16–20.

Turner, Martin, and Rachel Baskerville. 2013. "The Experience of Deep Learning by Accounting Students." *Accounting Education* 22, no. 6 (December): 582–604.

Wiggins, Grant. 1989. "Teaching to the (Authentic Test)." *Educational Leadership* 46, no. 7 (April): 41–47.

Yen, Jion Liou, and Kevin Hynes. 2012. "Authentic Assessment Validation: A Heuristic Rubrics Cube." In *Handbook on Measurement, Assessment, and Evaluation in Higher Education,* edited by Charles Secolsky and D. Brian Denison, 423–37. New York: Routledge.

Yunker, Barbara D. 1999. "Adding Authenticity to Traditional Multiple Choice Test Formats." *Education* 120, no. 1 (Fall): 82–87.

2

Authentic Assessment in Academic Libraries

Where Are We Now?

As we have seen, the concept of authentic assessment in a variety of forms has been around for almost thirty years, though higher education has been somewhat slower to implement it than primary and secondary education. In academic libraries, the conversation about authentic assessment has increasingly progressed over the past ten years, moving from discussions of the advantages and disadvantages of testing versus performance and other authentic assessments (Oakleaf 2008) to descriptions of authentic assessment techniques in relation to the ACRL framework (Oakleaf 2014), and moving toward explanations of how to put specific methods into practice. During that time, academic libraries have adopted a variety of authentic assessment techniques, although we should be clear that these approaches might be better adapted to some instructional environments than to others. For example, librarians who teach semester-long, credit-bearing courses, whether required or optional, can implement a number of authentic assessments over the course of several months, and the measures they use more closely resemble those used in discipline-specific courses. Because library instruction modes vary widely and include one-shot sessions, embedded librarianship (both in person and online), collaborations with faculty, tiered information literacy programs (both semester-long and over multiple years), and many others, the authentic assessments used within each setting can differ significantly. This chapter will provide an overview of where authentic assessment currently stands within the most common instructional settings.

CREDIT-BEARING COURSES

Many instruction librarians are fortunate enough to teach semester-long courses, either required or optional, for which students earn credit. These courses can assume many forms, but what they all have in common is the instruction librarians' ability to implement more authentic assessment techniques throughout the course of the semester. Much like credit-bearing courses taught by discipline-specific faculty, librarians who teach credit-bearing information literacy courses employ both formative and summative assessments. Formative assessment can be thought of as "small, frequent, and often informal assessments designed to help the educator get an understanding of students' current knowledge and what they have learned," while summative assessments are a "summation of what students have learned after the fact" (Broussard, Hickoff-Cresko, and Oberlin 2014). Having access to both types of assessment allows librarians teaching credit-bearing courses to gauge student learning using a wide array of measures that can help them to more authentically assess student learning than is often the case in other instructional settings. There are three main types of credit-bearing information literacy courses: course-integrated, discipline-specific, and library-specific. Within course-integrated and discipline-specific library classes, the course content is closely tied to a particular area or program of study, which can include subjects like English, business, and the STEM subjects as well as programs of study such as Honors. Library-specific courses are library research–centric and focus on developing higher-level library skills applicable to any subject or program of study. Librarians have used a number of authentic assessment techniques in both types of courses.

Over the past two decades, course-integrated and discipline-specific credit-bearing information literacy courses have implemented several different authentic assessment methods, both semester-long measures and shorter measures employed during the semester. For example, Ilana Stonebraker and Rachel Fundator report on a "longitudinal performance assessment" used to measure business information literacy after two required, semester-long one-credit classes required of management students at a large public university in the Midwest (Stonebraker and Fundator 2016). In order to measure performance across both semesters, students took the same online pre-test and post-test survey at three points throughout both courses. This performance survey measured the students' ability to retain information over time, and the study concludes that this type of measure provides more insight into both learning and retention since it assesses the long-term impact of credit-bearing library instruction classes. Along with this type of longitudinal assessment, librarians teaching course-integrated or discipline-specific credit-bearing information literacy courses use a number of different authentic assessment methods. These assessments include research portfolios that collect a student's work throughout the semester in order to document the search process and evaluation strategies. Portfolios can include documentation of resource selection and search techniques, with evaluative information that includes a student's assessment of both the relevance and applicability to their projects of the materials chosen along with their credibility and authority. In this case, a crucial component might also include a reflection in which the student explains why the information selected is deemed trustworthy. Research portfolios allow instructors to gather material from throughout the semester in order to gauge student progress and measure learning in a more authentic way.

Along with summative assessments such as research portfolios, discipline-specific credit-bearing information literacy courses employ additional formative assessment methods that can include performative task-based assignments (also known as performance assessments), quizzes, and short reflections as well as final projects such as longer writing assignments and annotated bibliographies. Performative task-based assessments ask students to perform a task rather than select answers from a list. In this case, an assignment might include tasks such as developing keyword searches, using those keywords to search a particular database or online resource, identifying appropriate reference entries or journal articles, and then listing the resources found, summarizing their contents, and presenting a short report that explains the process and results. In addition, credit-bearing courses allow instructors to assign tasks that build on previous assignments, scaffolding the information into manageable chunks throughout the semester. Quizzes can also be task-based and have the advantage of providing a snapshot of student learning at a specific point in time. In this case, in order to qualify as authentic assessments, quizzes should not include multiple-choice or true-false questions, since asking students to select answers from a set list tends to measure short-term memory and test-taking ability more than actual learning. Instead, quizzes can include components such as limited tasks, in which students are required to apply knowledge, or short answers, in which students reflect on their learning. Brief tasks can help instructors measure whether students have learned the course content and can apply their new knowledge in a relevant way. Short reflections employ metacognitive strategies in which students are encouraged to think about their own thinking and learning, which has been shown to increase "students' abilities to transfer or adapt their learning to new contexts and tasks" (Chick 2017).

Instructors in credit-bearing information literacy classes often use writing assignments and annotated bibliographies as larger final projects in order to ascertain students' ability to synthesize their learning and apply it in a more substantial way than in task-based assignments or on quizzes. While annotated bibliographies require students to conduct informed library research to locate appropriate material that builds on earlier task-based assignments, they also require that students reflect on the material they have found. Annotated bibliographies require students to synthesize information, summarize it, evaluate it, and provide a concise analysis in which they reflect on whether a particular source fits into their research, how they might use it to shape an argument, or whether or not it has changed the way they think about a topic. Writing assignments such as research papers require students to go one step further than annotated bibliographies. Annotated bibliographies can provide a foundation for a research paper in that students have already located, evaluated, and analyzed their sources, which can serve as a road map toward a larger paper that requires them to formulate a thesis and shape an argument based on those sources. In discipline-specific credit-bearing information literacy courses, research papers have the added advantage of connecting library research directly with the subject matter that students are studying, which can also help promote knowledge transfer in a more authentic way. That said, all of these methods ask students either to analyze, synthesize, or apply what they have learned, and in some cases, the assignment asks them to do all three. For example, portfolios can enable both students and librarians to see their work throughout the semester within a larger context that allows librarians to measure students' performance over time and allows students to reflect on their own learning in a different way. In addition, task-based assignments ask students to apply what they have learned, reflections ask them to analyze what they have learned, and both writing assignments and annotated bibliographies measure all three skills.

Library-specific credit-bearing courses have also developed authentic assessments for use throughout the semester, many of which either are the same or quite similar to those used within the course-integrated and discipline-specific contexts. These methods include pre- and post-test surveys; portfolios; research papers, projects, and presentations; annotated bibliographies; reflections; and quizzes and tests. However, while many of the measures used in both discipline-specific and library-specific credit-bearing courses are quite similar, the context in which they are employed can have a dramatic effect on both the students' estimation of the value of the information being conveyed and the learning that takes place. It has long been known that students tend to retain more information in course-integrated library instruction, since the information is, ideally, being conveyed to the students at their own point of need and as a means to a desired end (passing a class). Along with point of need, for more than thirty years librarians have known that information literacy "taught as a cognitive strategy" (Kohl and Wilson 1986), as opposed to mechanistic tool-based instruction, improves the quality of student bibliographies. Authentic assessments in credit-bearing courses allow instructors to combine all of these factors. For example, in library-specific credit-bearing courses, students are motivated to pass the class, which makes all of the information relevant to them. Employing authentic assessment instruments such as annotated bibliographies, written assignments, and reflections allows instructors to teach cognitive strategies that result in improved coursework and, perhaps, facilitate knowledge transfer from one setting to the other. Since "the capacity to transfer skills and knowledge provides a foundation for academic success," it is important that libraries contribute to "the development of foundational academic skills" in order to remain central to the institutional mission (Kuglitsch 2015). Authentic assessments in credit-bearing courses allow librarians the space and time to teach the cognitive strategies that help students develop key foundational academic skills as well as tell a more detailed story about the importance of the library for student learning.

EMBEDDED LIBRARIANSHIP

Embedded librarianship can take a number of forms; however, regardless of setting, embedded librarians are generally co-located, physically or virtually, within either a group or team. Embedded librarians "assume the role of team member" and "take on the same responsibility for team outcomes that other members share" (Shumaker 2012). In an academic setting, embedded librarians are usually fully integrated into a discipline-specific course and are not only aware of the learning outcomes of that course but as members of the team also bear some responsibility for student achievement of those outcomes. Much like librarians who teach credit-bearing courses, embedded librarians work with a particular class during an entire semester, in subjects ranging from first year writing to culinary arts, which allows them to employ more than one assessment instrument during that time. Librarian embeddedness ranges from the provision of one or two library instruction sessions, drop-in hours, and appointments to being present during every class period, leading discussions, and teaching up to five library-specific classes during the semester. The level of embeddedness drives the number of assessments librarians can employ, with fully embedded librarians able to assign pre- and post-test surveys, task-based worksheets, student reflections, and quizzes. In addition to these formative library-specific assessments, embedded librarians often have access to discipline-specific summative coursework such as research papers, annotated bibliographies, and capstone projects, which can provide a window into student progress as well as the librarian's contribution to that progress.

In order to supplement their evaluation of student coursework, embedded librarians have implemented a number of authentic assessment instruments that can help ensure that they are meeting their team's goals and contributing to course learning outcomes. Along with the instruments themselves, many librarians have also created scoring rubrics in order to ensure consistency in measuring student achievement. The most common authentic assessments employed by embedded librarians include student reflections and performative task-based assignments. Within this context, librarians often assign a reflection toward the end of the course so that students have a chance to look back at the arc of their progress from beginning to end. In order to help them frame this progress, librarians can provide students with a series of questions, or prompts that help them think about some of the important learning milestones that they have achieved. A standard set of questions also enables librarians to develop scoring rubrics, which are especially useful when they are embedded into entire programs rather than single courses. Rubrics are "a set of criteria for students' work that includes descriptions of levels of performance quality on the criteria" (Brookhart 2013). Well-designed rubrics should provide the kind of meaningful feedback that is important for authentic assessment and turns assessment into a tool for deep learning. This kind of feedback can help students learn more effectively by providing them with clear expectations of both the instructor and the student. For embedded librarians who need to assess a common assignment, rubrics allow for more uniformity in evaluation from one course section to the other. This kind of scoring aid can be especially useful when instructors ask students to respond to open-ended questions such as how their research process has changed over the course of the semester, how they evaluate and select sources, or how what they learned about library research might be transferrable. A rubric that defines the required components of each answer provides students with a common set of expectations and instructors with a tool to provide evaluation that is more consistent.

Student reflections and performative task-based assignments with scoring rubrics can be especially useful for authentic assessment of information literacy in embedded librarianship. Authentic assessments like these can help embedded librarians to measure a student's progress over time. For example, many embedded librarians provide several instruction sessions to each class during the course of the semester. However, it would be very difficult to measure their impact on student learning using summative coursework alone, since faculty assign that coursework and it reflects course content rather than library content. For example, without having a sample of a student bibliography created prior to library instruction (a pre- and post-test bibliography, so to speak), it can be difficult to gauge the level of progress any student has made, even with multiple instruction sessions. Without employing additional library-specific assessments, sorting out the librarian's impact on student learning would be challenging, if not impossible, which would mean that the librarian's contribution might go unnoticed. Given both the opportunities and challenges of embedded librarianship, authentic assessment not only helps librarians measure student learning in a more significant way but also, much like in credit-bearing courses, helps tell a meaningful story about the importance of librarians in a student-centered academic environment.

COLLABORATIONS

As information literacy increasingly becomes a common learning outcome in both general education and discipline-specific curricula, librarians have had more opportunities to collaborate with faculty in a systematic way. These collaborations have taken many forms, from working together on the design and sequencing of course assignments to fully co-teaching a course. In all of these situations, librarian participation goes well beyond embedded librarianship. Even though embedded librarians act as team members, they still perform a supportive role during the course—for example, providing discrete instruction sessions within a finite number of class sessions or maintaining a virtual presence in an online course module. When librarians co-teach a class, they are coequal instructors, are present during every class, and design and grade many of the assignments. Along with fully co-teaching courses, librarians have also collaborated on curriculum design, particularly in first-year writing courses where library research is built into the structure of the course from the first class meeting forward. In this case, librarians have also been able to design, administer, and grade assignments.

Librarians co-teaching courses employ authentic assessment instruments in a way that more closely resembles those implemented in credit-bearing classes, since the semester-long time frame provides opportunities for both formative and summative assessment. Librarians who collaborate with faculty on designing individual assignments or entire curricula are able to include library-learning outcomes more organically into subject-based assignments, so that those assignments serve two purposes.

Collaboratively designed assignments often ask students to perform tasks that measure the kind of real-world skills and abilities that can be crucial for authentic assessment. For example, students can be presented with a realistic scenario related to the performance of a specific task that might require them to do research within a professional environment, such as business, journalism, and health care, once they graduate. With the faculty member identifying the task and the librarian identifying the information literacy skills and abilities students might need to complete that task, the collaborators can develop an assignment that ties library learning more closely to subject-specific content, validating the importance of research skills and facilitating knowledge transfer. In addition, with information literacy increasingly named as a college-wide learning outcome, librarians who collaborate on curriculum development also have the opportunity to help craft institutional learning outcomes and weigh in on the design of authentic assessment instruments such as writing assignments that integrate information literacy skills into the research and writing process. Along with task-based assessments and individual writing assignments, faculty and librarians have also collaborated on developing rubrics for and scoring writing portfolios based on criteria important to both. Additionally, faculty and librarians have collaborated on developing peer evaluation techniques, whether in groups, on panels, or during discussion sessions. In all of these cases, students are encouraged to evaluate their peers' use and assessment of information sources in, for example, annotated bibliographies and research papers and to provide constructive feedback, which enables them to help their fellow students as well as to reflect more deeply on their own research skills.

Librarians who co-teach a course both help develop authentic assessments and integrate them into coursework and also work closely with students in order to identify research topics, develop annotated bibliographies, and use their sources to construct final papers or presentations. As a co-teacher, the instruction librarian more thoroughly understands the course content, not just from the syllabus or assignments but also from being present during lectures, class discussions, and student presentations. This presence allows the librarian to arrive at a deeper understanding of how much students retain from library instruction, how they use the information they have found, and where they need additional help. Along with that benefit, a consistent presence during class time validates the librarian's role as teacher, which increases the importance of library content since students need to master that content in order to complete the course successfully. In addition, collaborating on course-integrated assignments more clearly associates library learning with discipline-specific content and provides a context for more authentic assessment. In this case, librarians not only use formative assessments like task-based assignments and student reflections but also grade research-based student coursework, provide meaningful feedback, and participate in summative assessment of the entire course. Co-teaching with a librarian can also provide faculty with new insight into the research process and students' ability to find, evaluate, and synthesize information as well as to use it effectively to construct an argument. This kind of collaboration offers both faculty and librarians the ability to assess student learning in a more holistic and authentic fashion.

INFORMATION LITERACY PROGRAMS

Information literacy programs differ from other instructional models in that they are sequenced, either within a single semester or periodically throughout a student's academic career; are designed to progress in sophistication; and are formalized and widely disseminated (ACRL 2012). In practice, information literacy programs generally include a mandatory number of instruction sessions to which faculty have agreed, either within a specific discipline or during a student's entire program of study. Each program is timed so that students are scaffolded up from basic concepts, such as types and sources of information, to advanced skills like evaluation and synthesis. Because of this structure, information literacy programs can employ a variety of authentic assessments throughout the semester or course of study. Tiered information literacy programs that take place periodically throughout a student's academic career, also provide an opportunity to assess a student's learning from college entry to graduation, using instruments such as pre- and post-test surveys. In addition, librarians teaching within the context of tiered information literacy programs often provide instruction to students working on large research papers or capstone projects and can develop rubrics for assessing this coursework that consider the entirety of the program and the levels of instruction received. Along with these learning objects, tiered information literacy programs have used portfolios to gather artifacts of student work as well as library-specific formative assessments such as reflections and task-based assignments, throughout the course of the program. At the end of the program, a rubric can be used to assess the entire portfolio holistically in order to measure student progress over time. Librarians teaching in tiered information literacy programs can also assess student learning during key stages of the program such as basic introductory instruction in first-year writing, beginning research methods in a major, and advanced research techniques in capstone courses, by sampling student work and using a rubric to score it appropriately for each level.

While scaffolded semester-long information literacy programs do not offer as many options for summative assessment, they still provide instruction librarians with multiple occasions to implement authentic formative assessments, including tools such as worksheets that ask students to perform a specific task. This type of in-class performance assessment can also include questions that are designed to measure higher-level learning outcomes such as developing research questions. Students complete the worksheets during class and librarians review them in real time in order to provide the kind of immediate feedback that facilitates learning. Along with in-class worksheets, librarians in semester-long scaffolded programs have collaborated with faculty on the design and scoring of writing assignments and annotated bibliographies that incorporate information literacy learning outcomes. Providing information literacy instruction more than once during the semester also allows more time for librarian-led discussions around topics such as evaluating sources, which not only reinforce class content but also enable librarians to provide meaningful feedback to students at their point of need. In addition, librarians can also integrate peer evaluation, in which students weigh in on each other's skills in finding information and evaluating sources, into semester-long information literacy instruction. Librarians who teach in both types of programs, whether tiered over the course of multiple years or scaffolded during one semester, often have the opportunity to implement several assessment instruments, which provide them with a more authentic picture of student learning.

ONE-SHOT SESSIONS

The one-shot session in which a librarian meets with a class one time during the semester is easily the most common information literacy instruction model currently in place in higher education. In addition to the instructional limitations inherent in meeting with a class only once for about one hour, that individual session may not even last for the entire class period. Faculty often have complete control over how long or short that one-shot session lasts. And even when information literacy is included as a learning outcome in first-year seminars and other required first-year courses, it is often left completely up to the faculty member to decide whether and how much to collaborate with a librarian in order to meet that outcome (Booth et al. 2015). These challenges for instruction also present equivalent challenges for assessment. As a result, many librarians providing one-shot sessions stick to tried-and-true methods, such as brief surveys, or forego assessment altogether when they have less than an hour to both teach and assess. In addition, even when administered, surveys can be of limited utility and often tell us more about how students feel—how happy they were with the class—than they do about what students learned. Since this type of assessment doesn't require students to perform a specific task or to reflect on their own performance, a survey administered at the end of an instruction session might tell us whether most of the students in the class could, at that moment, differentiate between source types or where to search for them, but it rarely offers a window into whether or not students retain what they were taught or can transfer it to other contexts. In addition, this type of survey rarely offers librarians a chance to provide any kind of feedback, real-time or otherwise.

These limitations of one-shot sessions are well known, have been long debated, and are a consistent source of frustration for librarians who teach information literacy. However, the discussion of authentic assessment within that context is relatively recent and began to accelerate toward the end of the first decade of this century (Oakleaf 2011). Over the past few years, many librarians have been able to implement innovative authentic assessments in one-shot sessions. For example, working closely with faculty, instruction librarians have designed performative task-based assessments that students complete outside of class after the instruction session. In this case, librarians then grade the assignments and return them to students in order to provide feedback on search strategies, evaluation, and more. Instruction librarians have also developed quizzes that ask students to complete specific tasks and answer questions—factual, evaluative, and reflective—that they complete in groups during the instruction session. This kind of group work can also serve as a point for peer evaluation, where students compare their search strategies and evaluative judgments with the others in their group. Task-based worksheets have also been employed during one-shot sessions to provide authentic formative assessment. While there are a number of formative assessments available to librarians who teach one-shots, the brief length of these sessions means that summative assessment is not always possible. However, search logs, in which students explain their search strategies and reflect on their information-seeking behaviors, have been used to provide a kind of summative assessment for one-shot sessions.

Combining worksheets and search logs into one exercise/assessment instrument allows librarians teaching one-shot sessions to gather both performative and summative authentic assessment data simultaneously. In this case, the worksheet portion of the exercise asks the students to perform a specific task or set of tasks. The search log at the bottom of the worksheet provides space for students to reflect on their performance of the assigned tasks and explain why they chose the search strategies or resources that they did. This type of worksheet can also prompt students to compare how their search strategies worked in different environments, such as two different databases, and discuss why they might use one or the other to complete an assignment. The advantage of this type of assessment within a one-shot session is that it serves as both an activity and an assessment. Students get hands-on practice and are encouraged to reflect on their process. In addition, librarians provide immediate feedback as the students complete the exercise, intervening if a student appears to be having trouble and correcting mistakes in real time. Librarians have also combined worksheets with minute papers in order to gather formative assessment data that is both task-based and provides for some degree of student reflection on their learning. In this case, the worksheet asks students to perform tasks such as identifying keywords and developing database search strategies, identifying appropriate library resources, and evaluating information sources. The minute paper, administered at the end of the class, asks students to answer one or two questions and then reflect on their answers. Unlike search logs, minute papers provide for only brief reflection and offer more of a snapshot than a summation of student learning. However, when one-shot sessions last for less than an hour or are conducted for large lecture classes, minute papers allow librarians to employ the kind of metacognitive strategy that can aid in knowledge transfer.

Along with assessments that combine tasks and reflections, librarians have also used worksheets as pre-tests and post-tests, asking students to perform specific tasks before the library instruction session and then again at the end of the session. In addition to the worksheets themselves, many librarians have developed rubrics that outline performance expectations and allow the instructor to provide meaningful feedback. Librarians who teach one-shot sessions have also developed authentic assessments by adapting teaching and learning strategies found in subject disciplines like business and science. These methods are especially useful for teaching large introductory lecture classes, since many of the techniques outlined in this chapter are somewhat labor intensive and not especially scalable. For example, many business classes are taught using the case method, which includes components that can be adapted to provide an opportunity for active learning and authentic assessment strategies such as task-based problem-solving exercises, group work, and immediate feedback (Martin 2015). In addition, student-centered instruction such as problem-based learning has become an increasingly standard pedagogy in the sciences. This technique can be adapted to information literacy in a number of ways, including performance assessment of students' ability to solve information problems directly related to their assignments. For example, students may have an assignment to write a profile of a local neighborhood. A librarian teaching a one-shot library instruction session for this class could have the students complete an exercise that asks them to answer three questions about that neighborhood and document their search process and the strategies they used to answer those questions. In this case, the students have a problem they need to solve—finding reliable information about a local neighborhood—and the exercise helps them fulfill an immediate need while simultaneously providing the instruction librarian with an authentic performance-based assessment. Moreover, given that one-shot sessions are still the most common mode of information literacy instruction, it is important to keep in mind that many authentic assessment techniques are available to librarians within that setting.

ONLINE INSTRUCTION

With the steadily increasing number of courses and programs that are taught online, librarians have also seen significant growth in the need to teach and assess information literacy in the online environment. There are two main types of online instruction delivery, asynchronous and synchronous. In asynchronous instruction, learning objects—such as video lessons and tutorials—are embedded into course management systems or are available via additional online platforms, and students complete these lessons on their own time. In synchronous instruction, students attend class together at set times, much like face-to-face classes, and receive the same content at the same time. Librarians provide information literacy instruction in both environments, whether by creating library-specific learning objects and tutorial modules, by offering individual synchronous sessions, or by teaching during class times. In addition to the differences in delivery, online library instruction is provided within a variety of settings including credit-bearing classes, embedded librarianship, and one-shot sessions, and in each type of class, instruction is delivered both synchronously and asynchronously. Both types of online instruction present assessment challenges that librarians have addressed in a number of ways and that are often similar to assessments used in face-to-face classes. Nevertheless, due to the varied settings and delivery methods, assessment of online information literacy instruction often consists of evaluation surveys, multiple-choice tests, or citation analysis, and hasn't changed much since Samantha Schmehl Hines surveyed 143 institutions about their assessment practices in distance education (Hines 2008)—that points to the growing need for more authentic assessment in online instruction.

Despite assessment of asynchronous online instruction tending toward embedded multiple-choice quizzes and tests, librarians can use many of the same online tools to employ short-answer responses that provide them with assessment that is more authentic. In addition, when these responses are graded in real time, students receive immediate feedback in the form of contextual help that enables them to correct and learn from their mistakes and librarians are provided with a record of each student's progress toward completion. Along with short-answer quizzes, librarians have also embedded problem-based activities into online tutorials, where students complete tasks, reflect on them, and receive feedback on their answers. In addition, librarians who have created asynchronous information literacy modules have also employed pre- and post-tests to establish a baseline and assess learning before and after students complete the module. This method can be adapted to include short, problem-based answers along with more typical multiple-choice questions. When students are required to complete online information literacy modules, librarians have the ability to assign more authentic assessment instruments, such as final projects that demonstrate a student's ability to apply the knowledge gained from the tutorials. While summative in nature, these final projects resemble performance assessment in that they require students to complete the kinds of real-world library research tasks that they will encounter in their subject disciplines.

Assessment of one-shot information literacy instruction sessions in synchronous online classes can adapt some of the same authentic techniques that are used in face-to-face classes. For example, librarians can upload task-based worksheets, including worksheets that combine tasks, search logs, and reflections to the course management system; have students complete the worksheets at the end of class; and have them return the worksheets by email to the librarian. Unfortunately, due to the nature of synchronous online instruction, students do not receive immediate feedback in the way they do in face-to-face classes, which means that instruction librarians need to take extra care to allow for questions and answers during the session and to provide meaningful feedback to each student after scoring the worksheet. In addition, students' proficiency with technology as well as their personal computing devices can have a major impact on their capacity to get hands-on practice during the session, which can limit their ability to perform specific tasks during or after class. For example, if a student's laptop or tablet has a small screen, they may not be able to have two effective browser windows open simultaneously and thus would not be able to follow along with demonstrated searches or complete brief tasks to share and discuss with their classmates. Possessing the same limitations as face-to-face one-shot sessions, synchronous instruction of this type imposes additional challenges, many of which are beyond the librarian's control.

Assessments in credit-bearing online information literacy courses closely resemble those used in face-to-face credit-bearing classes, with a mix of formative and summative assessment techniques that include student reflections, peer evaluation, discussion boards, task-based assignments, writing assignments, and annotated bibliographies. Interestingly, these methods are used in both synchronous and asynchronous instruction, with students completing the assignments after viewing the course's instructional materials. These materials range from librarian-created slide shows, videos, and audio clips to online tutorials created by vendors that provide basic how-to instructions for searching specific databases. As in traditional credit-bearing courses, librarians teaching online credit-bearing classes have access to a wide range of authentic assessment techniques and can more easily measure students' progress over time. However, authentic assessments are still available to librarians teaching within a wide variety of online environments and instruments can often be adapted from face-to-face instruction, depending on setting, method, or need.

OTHER SETTINGS

While authentic assessments are rarely employed outside of formal library instruction, some librarians have been able to implement authentic assessments of student learning in other library settings, including at the reference desk and in library orientations. For example, librarians have used questions asked at the reference desk as a supplement to pre- and post-tests, measuring student progress by asking for demographic information such as whether or not a student had attended a library instruction session, and then mapping the type of question asked to attendance and level of sophistication (Cordell and Fisher 2010). Librarians have also developed activities and assessments for use in library orientations that generally provide a basic introduction to the library and include less instructional content than course-integrated information literacy sessions. For example, orientations can include an activity that serves as a performance assessment in which students are required to answer questions about the tasks they completed. Some librarians have also developed an ethnographic approach to orientation that includes mapping activities and guided focus groups as formative assessment (Pashia and Critten 2015). These focus groups involve both student discussions and immediate feedback from librarians. Problem-based learning activities with assessment rubrics have also been employed in library orientations, allowing students to explore the physical and virtual space and solve real-world problems related to it. Librarians have also assigned homework that requires students to creatively synthesize what they learned from the orientation activity. In each of these situations, authentic assessment has been incorporated into activities that often include no assessment components at all or, in the case of orientations, have generally taken the form of multiple-choice quizzes and general satisfaction surveys.

Table 2.1. Authentic Instrument by Instructional Setting

Credit-Bearing Courses	Embedded Librarianship	Collaborations	Information Literacy Programs	One-Shot Sessions	Online Instruction	Other Settings
Annotated bibliographies	Annotated bibliographies	Annotated bibliographies	Peer evaluation	Minute papers	Annotated bibliographies	Guided focus groups
Performative task-based assignments	Performative task-based assignments	Peer evaluation	Performative task-based assignments	Performative task-based assignments	Discussion boards	Performative task-based assignments
Portfolios	Pre-/post-tests	Performative task-based assignments	Portfolios	Problem-based activities	Performative task-based assignments	Problem-based activities
Pre-/post-tests	Quizzes	Portfolios	Pre-/post-tests	Quizzes	Pre-/post-tests	
Presentations	Reflections	Writing/research assignments	Writing/research assignments	Reflections	Problem-based activities	
Quizzes	Writing/research assignments			Search logs	Proficiency projects	
Reflections					Quizzes	
Tests						
Writing/research assignments						

SUMMARY

Overall, there are probably as many different types of authentic assessment available to instruction librarians as there are contexts in which librarians teach. As information literacy librarians move away from mechanistic instruction to engage with the ACRL Framework for Information Literacy, assessment has also begun to move away from multiple-choice quizzes and satisfaction surveys to more authentic methods of evaluating student learning. Tables 1 and 2 outline some of the most frequently used authentic assessment techniques, the type of assessment, and the settings in which they are employed.

While credit-bearing courses, embedded librarianship, and tiered information literacy programs clearly provide the greatest number of opportunities to implement a number of authentic assessments, it is important to remember that many of these techniques can be adapted to face-to-face one-shot sessions, online one-shot sessions, and asynchronous information literacy modules. Because one-shot sessions are the most common mode of information literacy instruction, achieving more authentic assessment of student learning in those sessions should be a primary goal for instruction librarians—not only because it is important to understand where instruction succeeds or falls short but also because it provides an opportunity to communicate the library's impact to key stakeholders in a more meaningful way. Moreover, despite the limitations imposed by one-shot sessions, authentic assessment of student learning in those classes is possible. The following chapter will provide an overview of the advantages and challenges of each type of authentic assessment within these instructional settings.

Table 2.2. Authentic Instrument by Assessment Type

Formative Assessment	Summative Assessment
Discussion boards	Annotated bibliographies
Guided focus groups	Portfolios
Minute papers	Pre-/post-tests
Peer evaluation	Presentations
Performative task-based assignments	Proficiency projects
Problem-based activities	Search logs
Quizzes	Tests
Reflections	Writing/research assignments

REFERENCES

Association of College and Research Libraries (ACRL). 2012. "Characteristics of Programs of Information Literacy that Illustrate Best Practices: A Guideline." American Library Association. January. http://www.ala.org/acrl/standards/characteristics.

Booth, Char, M. Sara Lowe, Natalie Tagge, and Sean M. Stone. 2015. "Degrees of Impact: Analyzing the Effects of Progressive Librarian Course Collaborations on Student Performance." *College and Research Libraries* 76, no. 5 (July): 623–51.

Brookhart, Susan. 2013. *How to Create and Use Rubrics for Formative Assessment.* Alexandria, VA: Association for Supervision and Curriculum Development.

Broussard, Mary Snyder, Rachel Hickoff-Cresko, and Jessica Urick Oberlin. 2014. *Snapshots of Reality: A Practical Guide to Formative Assessment in Library Instruction.* Chicago: Association of College and Research Libraries.

Chick, Nancy. 2017. "Metacognition." *CFT Teaching Guides.* https://cft.vanderbilt.edu/guides-sub-pages/metacognition/.

Cordell, Rosanne M., and Linda F. Fisher. 2010. "Reference Questions as an Authentic Assessment of Information Literacy." *Reference Services Review* 38 (3): 474–81.

Hines, Samantha Schmehl. 2008. "How It's Done: Examining Distance Education Library Instruction and Assessment." *Journal of Library Administration* 48 (3–4): 467–78.

Kohl, David F., and Lizabeth A. Wilson. 1986. "Effectiveness of Course-Integrated Bibliographic Instruction in Improving Coursework." *RQ* 26, no. 2 (Winter): 206–11.

Kuglitsch, Rebecca Z. 2015. "Teaching for Transfer: Reconciling the Framework with Disciplinary Information Literacy." *portal: Libraries and The Academy* 15, no. 3 (July): 457–70.

Martin, Lisa. 2015. "Assessing Student Learning during Information Literacy Sessions for Large Business Classes." *Journal of Business and Finance Librarianship* 20, no. 4 (October–December): 330–38.

Oakleaf, Megan. 2008. "Dangers and Opportunities: A Conceptual Map of Information Literacy Assessment Approaches." *Portal: Libraries and the Academy* 8, no. 3 (July): 233–53.

———. 2011. "Are They Learning? Are We? Learning Outcomes and the Academic Library." *Library Quarterly* 81, no. 1 (January): 61–82.

———. 2014. "A Roadmap for Assessing Student Learning Using the New Framework for Information Literacy for Higher Education." *Journal of Academic Librarianship* 40, no. 5 (September): 510–14.

Pashia, Angela, and Jessica Critten. 2015. "Ethnography as Pedagogy in Library Orientations." *Journal of Information Literacy* 9, no. 2 (December): 84–93.

Shumaker, David. 2012. *The Embedded Librarian: Innovative Strategies for Taking Knowledge Where It's Needed.* Medford, NJ: Information Today.

Stonebraker, Ilana R., and Rachel Fundator. 2016. "Use It or Lose It? A Longitudinal Performance Assessment of Undergraduate Business Students' Information Literacy." *Journal of Academic Librarianship* 42, no. 4 (July): 438–44.

3

Authentic Assessment Instruments

Advantages and Challenges

While librarians use an array of both formative and summative authentic assessment techniques within information literacy instruction, these methods can vary fairly widely based on the instructional setting in which they are employed. The selection of an appropriate assessment instrument depends on the nature of that setting, including duration, number of sessions, and much more. In addition, each method of authentic assessment brings with it both advantages and challenges. Since true authentic assessment asks students to synthesize, analyze, and apply what they have learned, it can be difficult to find a method that achieves all of those goals, particularly when instruction librarians have very little time in which to teach and assess. Thus, librarians need to evaluate both the setting in which they intend to implement authentic assessment and the individual instruments themselves in order to select a method that works best for their particular situation. This chapter will provide an overview of the advantages and challenges of the most common authentic assessment instruments in order to aid in that selection.

FORMATIVE ASSESSMENT

Discussion Boards

Discussion boards can be a very useful form of authentic assessment when instructors assign a task beforehand and then pose questions that ask students to reflect on their performance of that task. Guided discussion can also enable students to provide feedback to their peers and enable librarians to provide meaningful feedback to students. This method is particularly useful in the online environment, especially for credit-bearing courses or for librarians who are embedded in online classes. These discussions can provide instructors with metacognitive teaching strategies that offer a great deal of insight into what students think about their learning and can allow students to learn from and teach each other. Moreover, this kind of peer learning and teaching is known to improve student learning in a number of ways, not least because students "reinforce their own learning by instructing others" (Briggs 2013). In addition, when a discussion board is combined with a task-based assignment or problem-based activity, it can include all the key components of authentic assessment.

However, discussion boards also pose some challenges. If instruction librarians do not work closely with a class for more than one session, students may be less motivated to take part in these discussions, especially if their participation is entirely voluntary. This is especially true if the discussion board itself is not part of their discipline-specific course page but instead resides on another platform outside of their course environment. Along with those limitations, the students who need the most help—both from their peers and from librarians—are often less inclined to complete additional tasks that have no bearing on their final grade, since, as we have seen, grades are sometimes all that motivates many students. All of these factors make discussion boards an unlikely mode of assessment for one-shot sessions or when library content is not fully embedded within a discipline-specific course, including its online environment. In addition, even when librarians are fully embedded into a course, providing meaningful feedback to each student can be quite time consuming, but for students to learn from that feedback it needs to go beyond mere praise or disapprobation. Instead, librarians need to take time to explain how and why the student either succeeded or failed at a task in a way that connects with both the performance of the task and the student's reflection on that performance. Since most instruction librarians work with several classes during the semester, providing that kind of feedback for each session might very quickly become overwhelming. Thus, discussion boards have distinct advantages for credit-bearing courses, online instruction, and embedded librarianship, but they would be a challenge to implement in other instructional settings.

Guided Focus Groups

Guided focus groups have advantages that are similar to discussion boards in that students reflect on their experiences and provide peer-to-peer feedback. Since librarians direct these focus groups, they can construct prompts to lead the discussion in specific directions in order to keep it on track and to ensure that students reflect on specific tasks or activities. Guided focus groups offer face-to-face instructors some of the advantages that discussion boards provide in an online environment. However, for this method to qualify as authentic assessment, these focus groups need to include a task-based assignment or activity on which the students reflect. For example, if a focus group of first-year students is convened and asked to reflect on their experience of the library without having had any real experience of it, their comments might make an interesting sort of pre-test but would not tell us anything real about their learning. In addition, since focus groups do not require students to reflect deeply, their ability to determine whether students can analyze and synthesize information is limited. Nevertheless, this method can provide librarians with additional insight into student perceptions when used in combination with specific tasks and activities within a library orientation setting. In this case, first-year students might be assigned as part of their orientation an activity that asks them to complete a library activity worksheet outside of class and then attend a focus group session in order to reflect on the relative ease or difficulty of completing that task. If used in this way, guided focus groups can provide a helpful supplement in a basic introduction to the library. However, this assessment technique is less useful within one-shot sessions in which librarians have a limited amount of time to teach higher-order skills, since it would allow very little room for both instruction and the completion of task-based assignments prior to the focus group. That said, if librarians are embedded or teach a credit-bearing course and have access to students for more than one session, guided focus groups can complement additional assessment instruments.

Minute Papers

Unlike discussion boards and guided focus groups, minute papers take very little time and can be used within almost any instructional setting. Because they really can be completed in just a minute or two, when the prompts are structured effectively these brief assessments can offer a window into what students have learned and the questions or difficulties they continue to have. That said, if the questions are too broad or are opinion-based rather than learning-based, minute papers really cannot be considered authentic assessments. For example, most minute papers ask students to list one thing they learned from the instruction session—but without asking students to complete a task prior to answering that question, there is no objective way to measure their self-reported new knowledge. Combining a minute paper with a task-based assignment or problem-based activity would make the information gathered from them far more authentic since the minute paper would add a reflection component that offers insight into students' experience in applying what they learned to a specific task. In addition, if librarians ask students to complete a minute paper at the end of an instruction session but provide no feedback, either during or after class, then instructors would fail to reinforce student learning as well as fail to answer continuing questions. In this case, the minute paper would provide very little real information about student learning, and what information it did offer would have little impact on knowledge transfer or deep understanding. However, providing that kind of meaningful feedback, either during or after class, could prove time consuming, especially for larger classes and those of shorter duration, which would mitigate the chief benefit of this technique. For example, instruction librarians often work with multiple sections of the same class as well as multiple classes each semester. In addition, while the number of instruction sessions provided by academic librarians has been trending significantly upward over the past decade (Primary Research Group 2014), the number of librarians available to teach them has increased at a much slower pace (U.S. Department of Labor Bureau of Labor Statistics 2015). Moreover, academic library hiring has actually declined (ACRL 2017), which has led to an expanding workload for a decreasing number of librarians.

Thus, while minute papers can offer a useful snapshot into how students experience library instruction, they are not truly authentic when used as stand-alone assessments and do not promote deep learning when no feedback is provided. However, librarians employing minute papers in this way can still glean some helpful information about their own teaching. For example, if an instruction librarian overemphasizes one particular tool, such as a database or an e-book platform, many of the students completing the minute paper will list that tool as the one thing they learned. If the instruction librarian meant the session to be broad-based and provide a thorough overview of finding, evaluating, and using a variety of information sources, minute papers could offer a useful corrective that helps librarians rethink lesson plans in light of the intended learning outcomes and the actual student responses. Used in this way, minute papers can aid in the development of learning outcomes that librarians can then employ effectively in the backward design (Wiggins and McTighe, 1998) of lesson plans. Once librarians identify key learning outcomes, they can align the questions asked in a minute paper with one or more desired learning goals depending on the amount of time available for assessment that would help ensure that this short, easily implemented tool includes some degree of authenticity.

Peer Evaluation

As we have seen, peer evaluation, also known as peer assessment, can be especially effective in helping students reinforce their own learning. If students complete a task-based worksheet during an instruction session and then work in pairs or groups to evaluate each other's work, the act of evaluation alone can deepen a student's understanding of the material. For example, if one student explains a search strategy or evaluative technique to another, that act of explanation allows the student to apply the kind of metacognitive skills that both clarify concepts and allow for knowledge transfer. In addition, peer evaluation provides students with the kind of immediate feedback that is crucial for authentic assessment. Along with those benefits, peer feedback is "beneficial to all students but especially for those who might fail to detect their own misunderstandings" as well as "for those who might overestimate their own understandings and capabilities" (Nicol 2014). This concept is especially significant when considered in combination with the day-to-day experiences of instruction librarians, where overconfident students fail to pay attention and take it for granted that they know all they need to know about finding and evaluating information. This phenomenon, described so clearly by Justin Kruger and David Dunning, is critically important to keep in mind when assessing student learning. Without the kind of feedback that corrects misperceptions in a timely manner, students may walk away from an instruction session thinking they already know what they need to know, only to discover later when a paper is due or a grade received that they are actually struggling to find the kinds of sources that faculty require. Because "the failure to recognize that one has performed poorly will instead leave one to assume that one has performed well" and can lead to a situation in which "the incompetent will tend to grossly overestimate their skills and abilities" (Kruger and Dunning 1999), incorporating peer evaluation into instruction sessions can help to overcome some of the difficulties inherent in helping students to understand what it is that they don't know.

However, despite all of these benefits, peer evaluation can sometimes be difficult to employ based on the length or type of instruction session. For this method to work effectively, librarians need time to teach and students need time to perform tasks as well as to evaluate their own performance and the performance of their peers. Librarians can limit the time allotted for peer evaluation or can structure the session so that students work in groups or pairs to perform tasks or complete problem-based activities, with peer evaluation incorporated into the tasks and activities. These groups or pairs might then report their results to the rest of the class in order to generate discussion. This type of activity could take place during the last fifteen to twenty minutes of a sixty-minute session, with the first forty to forty-five minutes devoted to instruction and hands-on practice. In any case, librarians will need to balance the time they need to teach crucial content with the need to provide feedback and generate discussion, since this type of peer interaction is often where significant learning takes place.

Performative Task-Based Assignments

When constructed effectively, performative task-based assignments can embody nearly every aspect of authentic assessment, requiring the students to synthesize the information they have been taught, apply that information to completing a task, and then analyze their performance of that task. When accompanied with meaningful feedback—either via peer evaluation or from teaching librarians—these assignments can tell us much about the search strategies and evaluative techniques that students retained as well as what they thought of their own learning. Instead of measuring a student's opinion of the librarian's teaching style or the temperature of the classroom, or even their own comfort level with library research, task-based assignments that include a reflection component tell us whether or not a student can complete an essential task as well as whether or not they understood the meaning and value of the task they were asked to perform. This last component is especially important because it activates metacognitive skills, prompting students to answer the "why" questions about their own processes and abilities. In addition, students will learn more from the exercise if librarians inform them in advance of performance expectations and provide them with timely comments once they have completed the task. Rubrics can be an especially useful tool when combined with task-based assignments, since they provide students with clear grading criteria that can be applied in a standardized manner and allow librarians to offer consistent feedback to every student.

Performative task-based assignments and performance assessments can be used effectively within a variety of instructional settings, but they are especially useful for credit-bearing courses, in tiered information literacy programs, and within embedded librarianship, since those contexts allow for multiple assignments that can be scaffolded by degree of difficulty. For example, if a librarian provides more than one instruction session during the course of a semester, each session can include a task-based assignment mapped to the ACRL Framework that addresses increasingly sophisticated concepts as the class progresses. These assignments can move from simple search-and-find exercises to complex evaluation of the information sources the student found, as well as how the student might use that source within a paper or annotated bibliography. Librarians can also use scaffolded assignments to inform their teaching, reinforcing concepts that students have trouble with and correcting common misperceptions. This feedback loop—from student to instructor to student—can promote deeper learning, better instruction, and assessment that is more authentic.

Unfortunately, though, most information literacy instruction takes place in an entirely different setting that rarely allows for multiple meetings with the same class. However, task-based assignments that include all three components can still be implemented in one-shot sessions. In this case, the instruction librarian can scaffold the instruction session itself so that students move through increasingly difficult tasks as the class progresses. After brief instruction, students can complete a task that corresponds to that instruction, recording their progress on a worksheet. As they complete each task, a librarian can provide instant feedback before progressing to the next task. In this case, librarians spend more time roaming while students complete tasks than they do lecturing or demonstrating searches. Instead, the instructor can use the obstacles students encounter and the questions they ask to reinforce the lesson. In addition, when a student makes a good point the librarian can credit the student and share it with the class as a form of peer teaching. Used in this way, the authentic assessment instrument becomes a learning tool that drives student engagement with the material, and rather than being employed at the end of a relatively short session it becomes the content of the session itself. If the final task on the worksheet is in the form of a reflection or search log, this type of assignment would include all of the attributes of authentic assessment and could be completed within a relatively short time.

While this method of authentic assessment can be used effectively in one-shot sessions, the type of hands-on instruction that it requires would limit its applicability with very large classes unless more than one librarian participates. In addition, for librarians who provide instruction for more than one section of a required class such as first-year writing classes and first-year seminars, offering meaningful feedback after class on each student's reflection or search log could take quite a bit of time, especially for librarians who teach up to twenty sections in a given semester. Along with time spent grading, task-based assignments require careful constructing so that the required tasks are relevant to the course itself and students are motivated not only to complete them but also to pay attention to getting them right. In this case, for a librarian teaching course-integrated instruction sessions for a number of different courses across an array of subjects, it can be time consuming to create customized task-based assignments for every course. Ideally, each of these assignments should reflect the information needs of the class so that the tasks remain relevant and the students leave the session with both specific skills and a more general understanding of how to think about information. Thus, prep time for each session would increase given the time it takes to create useful assignments that meet all of these criteria. However, because this type of assessment provides rich information on student learning that can be measured over time, its advantages more than likely outweigh its challenges.

Problem-Based Activities

Problem-based activities include many of the same advantages and challenges found in performative task-based assignments. Like assignments in which students need to apply their knowledge in order to complete specific tasks, with problem-based activities students need to apply their knowledge in order to solve an information problem, ideally a problem that has a real-world component and is closely related to the subject discipline. However, unlike task-based assignments, problem-based activities can be more easily scaled up for larger classes, even large lecture sections, and can be used in a variety of instructional settings. Problem-based learning has been used most commonly in STEM disciplines, where students are presented with problems that "describe situations in which more than one approach could be used and in which alternative solutions are possible" (Svinicki and McKeachie 2014). Similarly, problem-based activities in information literacy instruction are used most often in course-integrated instruction for the STEM disciplines, business, and health sciences. Much like the instructional method used in the sample one-shot session for task-based assignments, instructors who teach using problem-based activities keep the lecture portion of the session to a minimum. Instead, the librarian provides a limited amount of instruction and then introduces a problem that the students need to solve, either by themselves or in groups. These problems differ from task-based assignments in that they are focused less on a specific skill such as identifying keywords or searching a database, and more on solving an information problem such as determining the best diet to achieve a nutritional goal, which would involve identifying appropriate source types, using sources to find information, and then evaluating their authority. Problems like this can be broken into parts in order to scaffold the students up throughout the session. At the end of the session, either individuals or groups can report out on their solutions. This method works well in large classes since students can work together to solve the problems and then designate one member of the group to report the results.

Problem-based activities tend to facilitate knowledge transfer since students are required to solve real-world problems that are applicable not only to their college courses but also to their chosen professions. In addition, if a reflection is incorporated into the activity and feedback is provided by the librarian, problem-based activities would include all of the components of authentic assessment. However, just as they have some of the same advantages as performative task-based assignments, problem-based activities also entail some of the same challenges, including the time it takes to customize authentic problems for multiple subjects, designing an activity that can be completed in a limited amount of time, and providing meaningful feedback to a large class. Ideally, a problem-based activity would be one of many assessments used within embedded librarianship, tiered information literacy programs, or credit-bearing courses. That said, they can still be used in one-shot sessions and scaled up to accommodate larger classes, which makes them an attractive option for incorporating relevant, authentic assessment into the library classroom.

Quizzes

Quizzes can be a useful assessment tool and are employed frequently in all types of library instruction from online tutorials to credit-bearing courses and one-shot sessions. However, quizzes that consist mainly of multiple-choice or true-false questions are not authentic assessments since they do not require students to synthesize, analyze, or apply their knowledge. Instead, multiple-choice and true-false quizzes that require students only to select answers from a set list or determine whether a statement is true or not measure only short-term memory rather than long-term learning. These types of quizzes are relatively simple to construct, can easily be embedded into asynchronous online tutorial modules, can be standardized and reused by multiple librarians, and can provide students with immediate feedback regarding the correctness of their answers, which makes them a popular choice for this type of instruction. In addition, quizzes in credit-bearing courses can provide a small window into a student's progress and, when combined with other assessment instruments throughout the semester, can help instructors understand what a student retains and what concepts might need more emphasis. Along with those benefits, quizzes can also be administered using a variety of platforms—from pen and paper to free polling applications to online library guides, and they can be completed quickly at the end of a one-shot session. In addition, online platforms allow librarians to administer quizzes and provide immediate feedback to a large number of students at the same time. With all of these attributes, it is entirely understandable that multiple-choice quizzes are the most widespread mode of assessment used by instruction librarians (Walsh 2009).

Nevertheless, if this type of quiz is the only assessment instrument used, it has limited value for assessing student learning unless it includes tasks that students need to perform. Because of that limitation, some librarians have developed quizzes that include components such as short tasks to which students apply their knowledge and short answers in which students reflect on their learning. Including these types of questions can help make quizzes a more authentic form of assessment. In addition, quizzes embedded into online tutorials that include short tasks, provide immediate performance feedback, and require students to revise their work before proceeding can reinforce student learning as well as provide librarians with a record of their progress through the module. Used in this context, a quiz can still be standardized and reused since it focuses on library content and is not course-integrated. However, authentic quizzes within course-integrated instruction require more customization since the short tasks need to be relevant to the subject content and learning outcomes, which obviates their transferability from one section to the next. Moreover, good quizzes that yield valuable assessment data can be time consuming to construct and grade, which negates another of their advantages. For those reasons, quizzes are employed most usefully in credit-bearing courses or other settings, such as embedded librarianship, where they represent one of several modes of assessment as well as in online library tutorials for which librarians develop one authentic quiz per module that is scored automatically.

Reflections

Reflections are valuable tools for prompting students to analyze and synthesize what they have learned in class. Reflections that "invite students to reflect on their learnings, to compare intended with actual outcomes, to evaluate their metacognitive strategies, to analyze and draw causal relationships, and to synthesize meanings and apply their learnings" (Costa and Kallick 2008) are not only an effective teaching tool but also provide instructors with an authentic mode of assessment. Much as we have seen with performative task-based assessments and problem-based activities, the act of reflecting itself is integral to student learning, and a reflection exercise in which students are prompted to answer well-designed questions functions as both an assessment and a learning object. In addition, similar to peer teaching and evaluation, reflections prompt students to explain complex concepts—in this case, to answer their own why questions—which can lead to the kind of higher-order thinking in which they make connections and apply their knowledge. Reflections can also help librarians improve their teaching practice by providing a window into how students actually experience instruction, what they take away from it, and any common mistakes and misperceptions that they may have. This type of tool can be much more valuable than, for example, a multiple-choice quiz, in that it provides librarians with a sense of a student's level of understanding rather than whether or not an individual's mind wandered during class or short-term memory failed at a given moment. Instead, when students reflect on what they did and why they did it, library instructors get a window into whether or not a student grasped an important concept and, crucially, understands why that concept is important.

However, effectively designed reflections employ guiding questions constructed to focus on the content covered during class. For example, a reflection that simply asks an open-ended question, such as "What did you learn in this class?" or "What did you think about library instruction?" will not elicit the kind of insight into deep conceptual understanding or demonstrate the application of new knowledge that is required for authentic assessment. In this case, instruction sessions that have been designed backward from a specific set of learning outcomes lend themselves particularly well to the use of reflections as a method of assessment. If those learning outcomes include typical basic skills such as constructing keyword searches along with higher-order skills such as evaluating information sources, students may need to perform certain tasks during the session in order to practice those skills. A reflection based on those learning outcomes can include questions focused on those tasks such as: "What keywords did you use to search for relevant information on your topic?"; "What types of information sources did you find using those keywords?"; "What type of information source did you find most useful for your project and why?"; "How would you use the information source (for example, it includes a helpful overview of my topic or situates it within historical context)?"; and "How do you know that the information you found is accurate (ask yourself who wrote it, who published it, and why)?" These types of questions can help students synthesize what they learned in class and then apply it to the tasks they performed. In addition, including prompts that guide the students (the "for example" and "ask yourself" questions), help them understand the most important points that they need to consider when analyzing how they find and evaluate information; this leads them to exercise higher-order thinking skills. It is always important to remember, especially for librarians who teach first-year students, that college-level library research is a big leap for most of them (Head 2013). Academic libraries offer an incredible array of resources across a wide variety of formats that can quickly become overwhelming for students who are still navigating being away from home or sharing a room for the first time. Thus, it is important to provide students with context for what we are asking them to do and why. Reflections that include guiding prompts help students contextualize and analyze both the task and its value. They also authentically assess whether or not students can synthesize, analyze, and apply what they were taught, even in a one-shot session.

Nevertheless, much like task-based assignments and problem-based activities, providing meaningful feedback on authentic reflections can be time consuming for librarians who teach a large number of students, and instructors will need to consider both the value of the assessment and the investment of time involved when deciding which formative assessment method to choose. That said, within the current higher educational context, the value of authentic assessment—in terms of both student learning and the library's ability to document its impact on that learning in a meaningful way—might perhaps outweigh the time commitment involved in designing information literacy instruction around authentic teaching, learning, and assessment. This question is especially crucial for librarians teaching one-shot sessions, which are often integrated into required first-year courses and involve the entire first-year class, and which are most likely not the only library instruction sessions that an individual librarian needs to provide during the semester. Moreover, while authentic formative assessments can be implemented in one-shot sessions, most authentic summative assessment may be out of reach, or of limited utility, within that setting. The next section will provide an overview of the summative assessments most commonly used in information literacy instruction as well as the advantages and challenges of each method.

SUMMATIVE ASSESSMENT

Annotated Bibliographies

Annotated bibliographies are a frequently used summative assessment technique, both in discipline-specific courses and within information literacy instruction. Annotated bibliographies have a substantial number of advantages since they are a true product of student work, can be scaffolded throughout a semester, and include all of the components necessary for authentic assessment. When paired with a grading rubric that sets performance expectations, annotated bibliographies can be a powerful tool for both learning and assessment. Because of their nature as summative assessments that measure the entirety of student learning during a course, annotated bibliographies are most commonly, and productively, used in credit-bearing information literacy courses (both face-to-face and online) and embedded librarianship. However, assessment of both annotated bibliographies and bibliographies from other student writing assignments has been discussed in the literature on information literacy instruction, including one-shot sessions, for quite a long time. And while it is interesting to have access to student bibliographies after they have had library instruction, it can be quite difficult to separate the effects of regular faculty instruction from library instruction. There is quite a bit of anecdotal evidence—from faculty feedback to student comments—that validates the positive impact of library instruction on student bibliographies, and it cannot be denied that many students do apply what they learned from a librarian to gathering, using, and citing sources. Nevertheless, direct evidence that could be used to communicate impact to the library's stakeholders is harder to claim. For example, without having access to a student's prior work—such as an earlier bibliography or first draft of a paper—the final product cannot really tell us much about the impact of library instruction on that student's performance. In addition, unless the paper or bibliography is due relatively shortly after meeting with a librarian, there might be weeks, or even months, that separate instruction from the final annotated bibliography. This situation is especially acute for librarians teaching one-shot sessions, since that session might occur relatively early in the semester and the bibliography might be due at the end of the semester. Sorting out the librarian's impact on that student's final work is both difficult to achieve and problematic to claim.

However, there are still several settings in which annotated bibliographies can be used to provide authentic summative assessment of information literacy instruction.

In collaborative teaching environments where faculty and librarians work closely together to design assignments and grading rubrics, and where the timing of instruction is closely related to the assignments at hand, annotated bibliographies offer one of the best methods both to evaluate student performance and to help students learn how to apply what they have learned in an authentic way. Moreover, if librarians gear their instruction to a specific learning artifact such as an annotated bibliography, the impact of library instruction on student performance may be more reasonably determined. In addition, in one-shot sessions that include an additional authentic assessment—such as a performative task-based assignment, problem-based activity, or reflection—both annotated bibliographies and general student bibliographies can be used as a supplement to the initial assessment instrument. Based on student performance on the initial assessment, the bibliography can be assessed to discern whether the instruction had a more long-term impact on the final assignment. In other words, did the students' performance on the annotated bibliography improve over their initial task-based assignment or echo their reflection? In this way, authentic formative and summative assessment would be available to librarians across most instructional settings, depending on the level of faculty-librarian cooperation.

Portfolios

Portfolios, which contain "a purposefully selected subset of student work," can be designed for a number of purposes, including highlighting "the progress a student has made," capturing "the process of learning and growth," and illustrating "the development of one or more skills with reflection upon the process that led to that development" (Mueller 2016). Portfolios are well suited for authentic assessment since they can include a wide range of learning artifacts, each of which demonstrates a different learning outcome. For example, instructors can select specific formative and summative assessments to include in the portfolio, such as a mix of task-based assignments, minute papers, and annotated bibliographies, which can then be graded holistically in order to demonstrate both the process of learning and its outcome. Holistic grading is often desirable because "analytic grading often fails to capture special characteristics, which properly managed holistic appraisals can" (Sadler 2009). In addition, portfolios that include reflections and self-assessments engage students with the types of "real-world" authentic skills that they will encounter in the workplace. However, because of their longitudinal nature, portfolios are rarely available to librarians outside of credit-bearing courses, collaborations, or tiered information literacy programs, though they have been successfully implemented in all of those library instruction settings. In each case, while portfolios brought with them significant advantages in terms of authenticity, they also entailed some significant limitations and challenges. For example, within tiered information literacy programs, in which more than one librarian provides instruction over the course of several semesters, or even several years, clear guidelines for both the material to include in the portfolio and rubrics for standardized grading can be challenging to develop and difficult to implement (Diller and Phelps 2008). If the material included in the portfolio fails to address the learning goals outlined by the rubric, then students may have difficulty understanding expected performance and instructors may have trouble assessing the assignments.

While necessary for assessing portfolios in a consistent fashion, rubrics can be especially challenging to develop within this context. For example, in some cases students might choose which learning artifacts to include in their portfolios. If so, instructors then need to develop a rubric for each potential artifact in order to accommodate every possibility and inform students of the performance expectations as well as how each artifact will be evaluated—which means that the rubrics need to be clear and concise for both students and teachers. In other words, students require a clear sense of how the rubrics are scored and why. In addition, within tiered information literacy programs and teaching collaborations, student portfolios ideally will be scored by more than one instructor in order to reduce subjectivity, which means that the scoring rubric should be designed to increase inter-grader reliability. However, if more than one grader assesses the portfolio holistically, as opposed to the individual learning artifacts it contains, conflicts in subjective judgments can occur between graders. Thus, it can be challenging to develop rubrics that include both analytic scoring and guidelines for holistic assessment that make sense to both students and instructors, since holistic rubrics "use extended verbal descriptions to set out the characteristics that are typical of, or expected for, each mark range or grade level" (Sadler 2009).

Along with the difficulties inherent in developing scoring rubrics for portfolios, providing consistent feedback that fosters student learning and improvement throughout the course of a tiered information literacy program can also pose a challenge. Ideally, library instructors would have access to the learning artifacts throughout the course of the program and would be able to assess and offer comments in order to promote more authentic student learning. In this case, ePortfolios to which librarians have access can provide a convenient location for both student work and instructor commentary. Nevertheless, ePortfolios can also present a technological barrier—for both students and librarians—if they are hosted on a separate platform outside of the institution's learning management system. Platform proliferation can create confusion and impede the learning of content since students have to learn how to use the technology before they can even begin to grasp the subject material. Along with the technical barriers—outside the setting of credit-bearing information literacy courses—negotiating librarian access to student portfolios can also pose difficulties if faculty are reluctant to collaborate not only on developing a multi-year information literacy program but also on sharing access to student work. However, as accrediting bodies have adopted information literacy as an important learning goal, colleges and universities have increasingly begun to list it among their institutional learning outcomes (Saunders 2011). Thus, a strong case can be made both for developing a programmatic approach to information literacy and for librarian participation in assessment of it as a learning outcome.

Pre-/Post-Tests

Pre-/post-tests are used extensively for measuring student-learning outcomes across a wide array of instructional settings since they provide teachers with a snapshot of a student's level of knowledge before and after instruction. Pre-tests provide instructors with a starting point that identifies student information literacy proficiency prior to instruction and can help to differentiate library instruction from discipline-specific learning, which allows librarians to tailor their classes in order to cover material that students do not understand. In addition, pre-tests can help instructors identify students who may need extra help or additional hands-on practice. Teachers administer post-tests to measure student learning after instruction. Post-test results can also be used to inform the development or revision of appropriate learning outcomes, as well as modes of instruction. However, as useful and ubiquitous as they are, pre-/post-tests are not without their drawbacks in terms of authentic assessment. For example, educators generally agree that pre-tests should be administered when students can be expected to have some knowledge of the topic being covered and so can be tricky to administer in the common first-year classes in which most librarians provide instruction. Given students' widely different experiences in secondary school, this situation can be especially pronounced if instruction is heavily weighted toward the first semester of the student's first year. While some first-year students will have had information literacy instruction at the secondary level, many students, particularly those most in need, will not have had any experience with it. In this case, if the pre-test scores were extremely low and so could only increase, then the post-test assessment would provide little useful information. In addition, educators also agree that for post-tests to yield any authentic assessment information they need to be administered at least twice, once at the completion of the individual class or course and again at a later date, in order to measure whether or not the students retained what they learned or can apply it. Thus, while some librarians have been able to implement pre-/post-tests in this manner to assess longitudinal performance, that option is rarely available within most library instruction settings. Moreover, most pre-/post-tests measure students' ability to retain facts rather than whether or not their ability to apply knowledge has improved. If a pre-/post-test is designed as a multiple-choice quiz or survey that requires students only to select answers from a set list, then the pre-/post-tests have the same drawbacks as any other quiz or survey that fails to require students to perform a task or to reflect on their performance.

Along with the difficulties involved in constructing authentic pre-/post-tests and administering them effectively, students often fail to complete all of the tasks in both the pre-test and the post-test. If an instructor designs the pre-test so that most students can be expected to know how to complete an assigned task, then they may be reluctant to complete what appears to be a repetitious task on the post-test. The reverse can also be true in that students might fail to complete an extremely difficult task on the pre-test but complete it on the post-test. Without including a reflection component that requires students to tell instructors why they did what they did, it can be difficult, if not impossible, to gather any real information about student learning in this way. In addition, well-designed pre-/post-tests are not only time-consuming to construct but can also be extremely time-consuming to administer, which makes them challenging to implement in one-shot sessions or other instructional settings in which time is limited. Nevertheless, pre-/post-tests can still be an extremely useful tool for authentically assessing student learning when librarians have the opportunity to work with students more than once during a semester or within credit-bearing courses and tiered information literacy programs. In addition, even when librarians mainly teach one-shot sessions, pre-/post-tests can be used productively outside the first-year instruction environment if first-year library instruction is mandatory. For example, many librarians provide course-integrated discipline-specific library instruction at the sophomore, junior, and senior levels. If it can be fairly assumed that those students have had baseline information literacy instruction, a pre-/post-test can be constructed to measure how much the student retained and can apply to that introductory lesson as well as measuring whether or not their skills improve after more advanced instruction. However, these same assumptions cannot be made when teaching graduate students since their experiences with library instruction can vary widely, from students who recently completed their undergraduate educations and experienced extensive instruction to those who are returning to school after a long absence and either had no library instruction during their undergraduate years or for whom library research has changed dramatically since then.

Presentations and Writing/Research Assignments

Presentations and writing/research assignments entail many of the same benefits and drawbacks as annotated bibliographies. While it can be challenging to differentiate the effects of library instruction from discipline-specific instruction, both methods include all the components of authentic assessment. Because of their nature as summative assessments, writing/research assignments, defined here as longer pieces rather than shorter artifacts such as minute papers, are most commonly employed in credit-bearing information literacy courses and embedded librarianship. In addition, because the advantages and challenges of writing/research assignments are so closely related to annotated bibliographies that have been previously described, a long discussion of their utility will not be included here. However, presentations are a useful method of authentic assessment that can be implemented within a one-shot library instruction setting. For example, if the content of a one-shot instruction session is geared directly to the skills students will need to master in order to create and give their presentations, then those presentations can act as a form of authentic assessment within that setting. As with annotated bibliographies, the length of time separating library instruction from a student's presentation is key to differentiating that content from what students learn in their discipline-specific classrooms. In addition, strong faculty-librarian collaboration can result in a presentation assignment that requires students to synthesize, analyze, and apply specific information literacy concepts in order to complete the assignment successfully, thus encouraging students to transfer skills from the library classroom to the discipline-specific classroom. Librarians can then attend presentations and use a rubric to score student performance based on each presentation's required components as well as more holistically in terms of a student's understanding of how to how to find required source materials and how well they used them to support their arguments. Moreover, the real-world nature and emotional immediacy of presentations can motivate students and encourage knowledge retention during the instruction session if they are able to directly connect library content to a high-stakes assignment.

As noted, this type of assessment requires strong faculty-librarian collaboration on both the learning outcomes and the assignment itself, either through codesigning it or through sharing it well ahead of the instruction session. In addition, based on the number of students, presentations may require a librarian to attend several class sessions in order to assess every student, which makes it difficult to implement with very large classes or with more than one class during the semester. Additionally, a class that includes a large number of students and meets only once a week can mean that some students give their presentations much closer to instruction than others do. This situation can have both positive and negative effects. On the positive side, students who present in later class sessions can learn from their peers by recognizing what worked and what did not for the earlier groups. On the negative side, while student learning may be improved by peer interaction, that experience can make it difficult to assess the impact of library instruction alone and might mean that the assessment data becomes increasingly skewed as the class progresses through the presentations. However, it would still be useful to compare how well students perform from the first class session to the last in order to determine whether performance varies significantly as the length of time between instruction and assignment increases. That said, the number of variables involved in creating a reliable measure—from the length of time between instruction and assignment to the effects of peer-to-peer learning—are beyond the scope of this discussion.

Proficiency Projects/Tests

Proficiency projects resemble performative task-based assignments in that they require students to complete specific tasks that require "hands-on demonstrations of key competencies to show how skills apply in real-world situations" (Lamb 2017). Proficiency projects are most often used in required and/or credit-bearing courses and have many of the strengths and weaknesses of task-based assignments. Tests also function as longer summative versions of shorter formative assessments such as quizzes. In both cases, well-designed tests and proficiency projects require students to demonstrate their ability to perform a specific task and to reflect on their performance of that task, which would thus require them to synthesize, analyze, and apply what they have learned in order to complete them successfully. These types of assessments can vary in their level of authenticity based on the included components, but they resemble each other in that they are difficult to implement in one-shot sessions since both assessments require far more exposure to information literacy content than one-shot sessions can provide. Proficiency projects can be implemented in other settings such as embedded librarianship and tiered information literacy programs, but the key factor is for students to attend more than one class on information literacy in order to allow librarians to scaffold their instruction. If the project requires students to have mastered multiple competencies, then multiple sessions will be required in order to teach them.

Authentic testing has long been discussed within all levels of education. This kind of test requires students to perform or exhibit their knowledge in a way that demonstrates their mastery of an "intellectual challenge" at "the heart of a discipline" (Wiggins 1989). In order for tests to qualify as authentic assessments, they require students not only to master a specific set of skills or to learn a specific set of concepts but also to put those skills into practice and demonstrate an understanding of the concepts behind them, combining performance with understanding. Essentially, authentic tests require students to enact their learning. And while librarians within a variety of instructional settings have employed tests (most often in the form of post-tests) as a form of assessment, given the length and nature of authentic tests they are infrequently used outside of credit-bearing courses. In that setting, instructors can employ a variety of formative assessments throughout the semester to measure student progress and provide ongoing feedback. Instructors can use those periodic formative assessments to inform test design in order to create a test that accurately measures the students' knowledge of course content as well as their ability to apply that knowledge. Like proficiency projects, authentic tests are most productively used in settings that allow instructors to scaffold course content over a longer period than is generally available to library instructors.

Search Logs

Search logs, in which students explain their search strategies and reflect on their information-seeking behaviors, are probably the form of summative assessment most available to librarians who teach one-shot sessions. Search logs can be used as both an assessment instrument and a teaching tool in that students get hands-on practice applying their knowledge to specific tasks and then reflect on their performance of those tasks. If search logs are integrated into the lesson plan, librarians can provide immediate feedback as students work through the exercise, intervening when a student struggles and correcting mistakes promptly. Similar to other assessments that require students to reflect on their learning, search logs activate metacognitive skills and provide students with a structure in which to think about their own thinking. Librarians can also use student search logs to improve their teaching practice in a more authentic way than can be obtained through minute papers or other similar techniques since search logs provide a record of what students actually did and why they did it. This information can help librarians gain a better understanding of what concepts students struggle with most, which can lead to rethinking and redesigning instruction sessions to concentrate on the key areas that students find most confusing.

Librarians can also use search logs to compare student performance over time that would serve as a form of longitudinal teaching assessment. If the same librarian teaches the same content from one semester to the next (such as, for example, an introductory class to first-semester first-year students), it is possible to measure the effects of any modification in methodology or change in learning outcomes by comparing student search logs before and after those changes. If we ask ourselves whether students continue to struggle with the same concepts or if they seem to have a better understanding after experiencing a modified lesson plan or the emphasis of a different learning outcome, that information can help us continually improve our teaching practice as we discover what appears to work and what does not. However, this type of teaching assessment cannot be used to compare instructors, since, even with standard lesson plans, teaching style can vary widely from one librarian to another. In addition, this type of assessment is best used when students have had similar experiences with library instruction, which can help sort out variable student skill levels and provide instructors with a better understanding of their own teaching effectiveness.

Finally, while there are a substantial number of formative and summative authentic assessment techniques available to librarians, most of them might appear to be difficult to implement, especially within the setting of one-shot instruction sessions. However, even though authentic assessment is more time-consuming and often more challenging to employ than traditional measures such as multiple-choice quizzes, the rich data it provides and the real student learning that takes place makes it a necessary and valuable teaching and learning tool. Thus, the next chapter will demonstrate how authentic assessment can be employed successfully across a wide array of library instruction settings.

REFERENCES

Association of College and Research Libraries (ACRL). 2017. "Academic Libraries." *State of America's Libraries 2017*. http://www.ala.org/news/state-americas-libraries-report-2017/academic-libraries.

Briggs, Sara. 2013. "How Peer Teaching Improves Student Learning and Ten Ways to Encourage It." *InformED*, June 7. http://www.opencolleges.edu.au/informed/features/peer-teaching/.

Costa, Arthur L., and Bena Kallick. 2008. "Learning through Reflection." In *Learning and Leading with Habits of Mind: 16 Essential Characteristics for Success*, edited by Arthur L. Costa and Bena Kallick. Alexandria, VA: Association for Supervision and Curriculum Development.

Diller, Karen R., and Sue F. Phelps. 2008. "Learning Outcomes, Portfolios, and Rubrics, Oh My! Authentic Assessment of an Information Literacy Program." *Portal: Libraries and the Academy* 8, no. 1 (January): 75–89.

Head, Alison J. 2013. "Learning the Ropes: How Freshmen Conduct Course Research Once They Enter College." *Project Information Literacy*. December 4. http://www.projectinfolit. org/uploads/2/7/5/4/27541717/pil_2013_freshmenstudy_fullreportv2.pdf.

Kruger, Justin, and David Dunning. 1999. "Unskilled and Unaware of It: How Difficulties in Recognizing One's Own Incompetence Lead to Inflated Self-Assessments." *Journal of Personality and Social Psychology* 77, no. 6 (December): 1121–34.

Lamb, Annette. 2017. "Debunking the Librarian 'Gene': Designing Online Information Literacy Instruction for Incoming Library Science Students." *Journal of Education for Library and Information Science* 58, no. 1 (January): 15–26.

Mueller, Jon. 2016. "Portfolios." *Authentic Assessment Toolbox*, July 1. http://jfmueller.faculty. noctrl.edu/toolbox/whatisit.htm.

Nicol, David. 2014. "Good Designs for Written Feedback for Students." In *McKeachie's Teaching Tips: Strategies, Research, and Theory for College and University Teachers*, edited by Marilla D. Svinicki and Wilbert J. McKeachie. Belmont, CA: Wadsworth, Cengage Learning.

Primary Research Group. 2014. *College Information Literacy Efforts Benchmarks*. New York: Primary Research Group.

Sadler, D. Royce. 2009. "Indeterminacy in the Use of Preset Criteria for Assessment and Grading." *Assessment and Evaluation in Higher Education* 34, no. 2 (April): 159–79.

Saunders, Laura. 2011. *Information Literacy as a Student Learning Outcome: The Perspective of Institutional Accreditation*. Santa Barbara, CA: Libraries Unlimited.

Svinicki, Marilla D., and Wilbert J. McKeachie. 2014. "Assessing, Testing, and Evaluating: Grading Is Not the Most Important Function." In *McKeachie's Teaching Tips: Strategies, Research, and Theory for College and University Teachers*, edited by Marilla D. Svinicki and Wilbert J. McKeachie. Belmont, CA: Wadsworth, Cengage Learning.

U.S. Department of Labor Bureau of Labor Statistics. 2015. "Librarians." *Occupational Outlook Handbook, 2016–17 Edition*, December 17. https://www.bls.gov/ooh/education-training-and-library/librarians.htm.

Walsh, Andrew. 2009. "Information Literacy Assessment: Where Do We Start?" *Journal of Librarianship and Information Science* 41, no. 1 (March): 19–28.

Wiggins, Grant. 1989. "Teaching to the (Authentic Test)." *Educational Leadership* 46, no. 7 (April): 41–47.

Wiggins, Grant P., and Jay McTighe. 1998. *Understanding by Design*. Alexandria, VA: Association for Supervision and Curriculum Development.

4

Authentic Assessment in Action

Once librarians have evaluated a variety of authentic assessment instruments and selected a technique that seems to work best within their instructional and institutional
context, it can be challenging to determine the best way to implement their chosen
methods. Thus, it can be helpful to gain an understanding of how each formative
and summative assessment instrument has been used across instructional settings in
order to get a clearer sense for how these methods have worked in actual practice.
As we have seen, the conversation around authentic assessment in academic libraries
has significantly increased over the past decade, and instruction and information literacy librarians have used a wide array of methods in order to better assess authentic
student learning. This chapter will highlight individual case studies that represent
authentic assessment in action to help librarians to develop an implementation plan
as well as to begin to understand what best practices for authentic assessment might
look like. This chapter does not intend to provide an exhaustive list of every use of
each authentic assessment instrument but rather to provide an overview of some of
the strongest uses of each technique.

FORMATIVE ASSESSMENT

Discussion Boards

Online instruction is the most common setting in which librarians have used
discussion boards as authentic assessment instruments. This instruction includes
both credit-bearing information literacy classes and embedded librarianship in
which librarians have a strong presence within a course learning management sys-

tem. For example, "librarians at Ball State work with many asynchronous classes. They often act as embedded librarians in the Blackboard course site, creating learning objects such as tutorials and LibGuides" as well as "facilitating discussion-board conversations" (Courtney and Wilhoite-Mathews 2015). Given the nature of asynchronous online instruction—particularly outside of credit-bearing courses—discussion boards can be the best way to generate real information about what students are learning, what they are struggling with, and what they think about their own learning. In this case, "within Blackboard, the librarian sets up a discussion board so that students could discuss what they learned throughout the semester about the research process. Also, students could post questions they have about research, and the other students and embedded librarian would respond as needed." This case is particularly interesting because the discussion board includes not only a reflection component but also peer-to-peer instruction, that, as we have seen, helps facilitate knowledge transfer. Allowing students to answer each other's questions helps reinforce their own learning by promoting higher-order thinking as a habit of mind.

Embedded librarians have also gone a step further and used discussion boards in online learning communities as a supplement to performative task-based assignments. For example, librarians at Chandler-Gilbert Community College designed an activity in which students were asked to "research a classmate's topic to find a relevant full-text journal article for him/her," after which the "students share their findings through the discussion board, including their search strategy, the article PDF, and their rationale for the article's relevance" (Burgoyne and Chuppa-Cornell 2015). This type of assignment helps to broaden the students' understanding of research as a process and also requires them to synthesize their knowledge, apply it to finding an article for another student, and analyze why they chose the article they did—all of which make it a truly authentic assessment. As an added bonus, this type of task-based discussion board also includes a peer instruction component. Along with peer instruction, librarians have also employed peer evaluation through discussion boards. For example, librarians teaching a credit-bearing online information literacy class at Hofstra University taught students how to evaluate the appropriateness of specific types of resources including books and journals. After instruction, students were assigned a discussion board activity in which they were asked "to discuss and evaluate any one criterion of the book, which the instructor did not evaluate," including "how well the book met the criterion. Students were then asked to respond to each other's posts, critiquing each other as to whether the book was appropriately evaluated on a specific criterion" (Catalano 2015). In this case, peer evaluation encourages students to reflect more deeply on their own learning process and provides teaching librarians with additional insight into how well students understood the concept of evaluative criteria, whether or not they could apply the concept to their own work, and how well they could explain it to each other.

Librarians at Duquesne University also used discussion boards in distance learning to provide nontraditional adult students with the kind of "peer-support that worked so well for the face-to-face sections." In this case, "throughout the semester, the librarian posted information to the discussion board about how to use the library," and "through the discussion board, the students could respond to the librarian's postings, ask the librarian questions, and respond to each other's postings as well" (Rapchak and Behary 2013). This peer support included responding to other students' postings much as students would respond to each other in a traditional classroom discussion. Along with facilitating peer support, the discussion board questions developed by librarians at Duquesne "were open and relevant to both coursework and real-world applications," which approximated a problem-based activity and prompted students to apply and transfer the knowledge they gained in the course. Asking students to "research urban legends or questionable medical advice" prompts them to think about how they would solve an information problem in any setting and encouraging students to discuss their resolution of that problem helps them gain higher-order critical thinking skills. Since class discussion is widely viewed as a vitally important learning tool that helps develop "students' reasoning skills because it gives you access to their thought processes and an opportunity to guide students to a higher level of thinking" (McGonigal 2005), online discussion boards can help facilitate that kind of thinking through and about solving information problems.

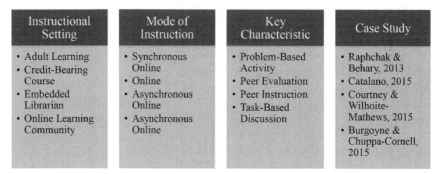

Instructional Setting	Mode of Instruction	Key Characteristic	Case Study
• Adult Learning • Credit-Bearing Course • Embedded Librarian • Online Learning Community	• Synchronous Online • Online • Asynchronous Online • Asynchronous Online	• Problem-Based Activity • Peer Evaluation • Peer Instruction • Task-Based Discussion	• Raphchak & Behary, 2013 • Catalano, 2015 • Courtney & Wilhoite-Mathews, 2015 • Burgoyne & Chuppa-Cornell, 2015

Figure 4.1. Method of assessment: Discussion boards. Jennifer S. Ferguson.

Guided Focus Groups

While guided focus groups to assess student learning rather than library services have been implemented less frequently than other formative assessments, they have been used to assess student learning in instructional settings that rarely include a formal assessment component, especially authentic assessment. For example, librarians at the University of West Georgia used a guided focus group exercise as their orientation activity. In this case, the instruction librarians met students in a classroom and "asked them to draw a map of the library on large whiteboards without any prior specific preparation" and a volunteer "was asked to draw what they saw in the library as they walked to the library session." After the maps were drawn, students were "asked to reflect upon their affective experience of the library space" (Pashia and Critten 2015). This discussion took the form of a guided interview, with the instructor prompting other students to add more information or to comment on the spaces themselves. This type of discussion helped the teaching librarian "address misconceptions and gaps in knowledge," encouraged the students to reflect critically on their impressions, and allowed for peer interaction and instruction. This technique allowed librarians providing a library orientation to engage students actively with the library as well as to gather real-time formative assessment information.

Librarians at the University of Huddersfield employed a similar ethnographic technique, cognitive mapping, in order to discover how a specific international student population interacted with the library and what they understood about library research. In this case, "students were to be given six minutes to draw a map of where they go to learn or study, either formal or informal space located on or off campus" (Sharman 2017). At the end of the six minutes, guided interviews were conducted. Students were asked to describe what they had drawn, and the interviewers used prompts "to find out what they included and what was left out, whether they worked in groups in the space or on their own and finally if they have a favourite place to go." This method can be particularly interesting when working with populations of international students who may have very different understandings and expectations about library research than students who went to secondary school or undergraduate college in Anglophone countries. In this case, having a baseline understanding of the needs of international students can prompt those students to undertake the kind of reflection on their own learning that may not have been required in their home country. The librarians at Huddersfield felt that the mapping and interview process "highlighted differences between the study culture encountered at their home institutions and what was expected in the UK" and that "none of the students interviewed were aware of the research help they can receive from librarians." This understanding about cultural and educational differences can help librarians begin to assess international student learning in a more culturally competent way.

Librarians at the University of Arizona have also used guided focus groups to assess the information literacy skills of incoming students—in this case, entering first-year professional pharmacy students. After attending a lecture by a librarian, the students were provided with five preliminary questions prior to participating in one of two fifty-five-minute focus groups. During the sessions, the librarians used nine open-ended questions to guide the discussions. The five preliminary questions asked for demographic information, including where students earned their undergraduate degrees and whether or not they had attended a library instruction session during that time. The nine open-ended questions included topics such as "If you were asked to conduct a literature review on a topic, how would you begin your search and where?" (Martin and Slack 2013), which not only allowed students to reflect on their own process and comment on other students' practices but also provided the librarians with insight into the students' prior knowledge and research habits. In addition, since the students participated in the focus groups after having attended a session on information literacy, these discussions also provided the librarians with a formative instrument that assessed what the students had learned in the library instruction session. Thus, the focus group offered the Arizona librarians two types of assessment—formative assessment of student learning plus a brief assessment of teaching effectiveness. Understanding what students learned during instruction can help librarians adjust their lesson plans in order to better meet learning outcomes. In addition, prompting students to reflect on their own learning helps promote higher-order thinking skills. Ideally, a library instruction session that includes a follow-up focus group would also include a task-based assignment or problem-based activity for students to apply their learning. The focus group would then supply both the critical reflection and timely feedback that are essential for authentic assessment.

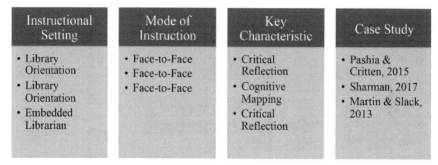

Instructional Setting	Mode of Instruction	Key Characteristic	Case Study
• Library Orientation • Library Orientation • Embedded Librarian	• Face-to-Face • Face-to-Face • Face-to-Face	• Critical Reflection • Cognitive Mapping • Critical Reflection	• Pashia & Critten, 2015 • Sharman, 2017 • Martin & Slack, 2013

Figure 4.2.   Method of assessment: Guided focus groups. Jennifer S. Ferguson.

Minute Papers

Minute papers are frequently employed for information literacy assessment. Because of their ease of implementation and the short time frame in which they can be administered, minute papers are particularly attractive for librarians who teach one-shot sessions. With some slight adjustments, minute papers can also provide authentic formative assessment. For example, librarians at the University of Mississippi reported on their use of minute papers for authentic information literacy outcomes assessment; they designed the minute papers as reflections and chose "questions that were directly related to the focus of the classroom sessions" (Choinski and Emmanuel 2006). These questions, for example, asked students to discuss why they might choose a specific resource to complete their assignments and asked them to evaluate specific information sources. As such, the students were prompted to synthesize what they had learned in class and apply it to completing the minute paper, which made this particular iteration more authentic than similar assignments that ask students about what they did or did not understand. Since, as we have seen, the students most in need of help are not always the best judges of what they know or do not know, minute papers that act more as self-assessments than reflections provide very little useful information about what students actually learned. Thus, this type of reflective minute paper provides more authentic data since students need to understand particular concepts to answer the questions. One of the most interesting aspects of the Mississippi librarians' minute-paper implementation is that students completed them outside of class after the library instruction session and turned them in to their professors with the assignments on which the instruction was based. At the end of the semester, the faculty members returned the minute papers to the librarians for scoring. The advantage of this method is that students directly relate completion of the library assignment to the completion of their course assignment, thus lending it more legitimacy and motivating students to complete it thoughtfully. The disadvantage of this method is that librarians cannot then provide timely feedback to students and answer any lingering questions that they might have. Nevertheless, minute papers designed in this way do allow librarians to authentically assess student learning after a one-shot instruction session.

Authentic minute papers have also been successfully implemented within the context of one-shot sessions and completed by students during class time. For example, librarians at East Carolina University employed a number of formative assessments as part of a comprehensive information literacy program for freshman writing classes. In this case, "the minute paper asks students to write about what they learned in a session" (Gustavson 2012). Interestingly, they also employed a similar self-assessment during some sessions and found that "students were more likely to use sophisticated library vocabulary in the Minute Paper . . . possibly because the Minute Paper required them to focus on one topic instead of three." At East Carolina, minute papers were used mostly as a reflection-based supplement in combination with task-based assignments that "include collected worksheets that review specific research abilities and task-oriented Activities." Used in this way, minute papers are both a learning tool and an authentic assessment instrument. In addition, librarians at James Cook University used minute papers in a particularly interesting way, where they served as a pre-/post-test instrument (Wolstenholme 2015). In this case, they designed two different minute papers, one labeled a polling one-minute paper (POMP) and the other a reflective one-minute paper (ROMP). The polling minute papers asked researchers (mostly postgraduate students and faculty or staff researchers in the sciences) to assess their understanding of a particular research topic. Unlike post-instruction self-assessments, the librarians distributed the POMPs one week prior to instruction and then used the results to design learning outcomes for the instruction session. At the end of the session, the librarians shared a link to the ROMP and had the researchers complete it during the session or directly afterward. The pre-/post-test nature of this use of minute papers addresses some of the key concerns about the use of minute papers as authentic assessments, since they helped librarians identify "what researchers understood or were doing well and also gaps in their current knowledge or activities." Understanding those gaps allowed the librarians to construct meaningful instruction sessions as well as to score the ROMPs for responses specifically related to the learning needs identified in the POMPs. As the librarians at James Cook University conclude, "POMPs allow researchers to benchmark the status of their learning needs and assist librarians to identify learning gaps. ROMPs encourage researchers to reflect on what they learned in library research support sessions and assist librarians to determine whether intended learning outcomes were achieved." In addition to gaining a better understanding of student learning, this use of minute papers can also help librarians improve their practice if the learning outcomes identified by the pre-tests are rarely accomplished.

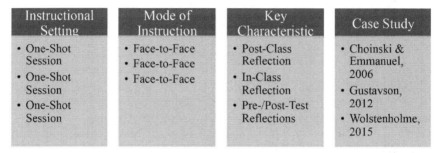

Instructional Setting	Mode of Instruction	Key Characteristic	Case Study
• One-Shot Session	• Face-to-Face	• Post-Class Reflection	• Choinski & Emmanuel, 2006
• One-Shot Session	• Face-to-Face	• In-Class Reflection	• Gustavson, 2012
• One-Shot Session	• Face-to-Face	• Pre-/Post-Test Reflections	• Wolstenholme, 2015

Figure 4.3.   Method of assessment: Minute papers. Jennifer S. Ferguson.

Peer Evaluation/Peer Instruction

Peer instruction can be a very powerful learning tool, and peer evaluation prompts students to reflect on their own learning, reflect on their classmates' learning, and apply standards to both. In order to evaluate the work of their peers, students need to be able to understand the task they need to perform, understand what competent performance of that task entails, and understand how to judge whether the task has been performed competently. In order to provide this kind of evaluation, students need to be able to synthesize information, apply what they learned, and analyze that application, which activates metacognitive understanding. Because peer evaluation is such a valuable learning tool, many librarians have employed it as a method of authentic assessment of information literacy. For example, librarians at Gettysburg College collaborated with faculty to provide a series of three instruction sessions to an upper-level course in public health and implemented a unique method of peer evaluation. In this case, they "staged a mock scientific review panel, modeled after the National Institutes of Health procedures." This panel "included both oral and written peer critiques, which allowed students to engage with each others' work, evaluating use and assessment of information gathered and synthesized by their peers" (Smith and Dailey 2013). The oral critiques provided students with immediate feedback on their presentations, while the written critiques prompted the students to synthesize their own understanding of the use of appropriate source materials in order to provide meaningful comments on each others' work. The librarians at Gettysburg found that "it was encouraging to see students note when their fellow classmates backed up their arguments with previous research." In addition, "in written peer reviews, several students critiqued their classmates for not fully developing their arguments with the most appropriate information, demonstrating that, as the reviewer, they were asking the appropriate questions." When students are able to ask the appropriate questions it demonstrates that they have achieved a deeper understanding of what it means to be information literate—moving from the mechanistic finding of information to higher-order evaluation. In addition, in the Gettysburg case the students were not only prompted to evaluate the quality of the information sources their fellow students used but also to provide feedback on how they used those sources to construct an argument, leading to a deeper understanding of scholarship as conversation by actively participating in the scholarly conversation themselves.

Librarians at the University of Auckland also used peer feedback to assess student learning in graduate and undergraduate Population Health research methods courses. In this case librarians used what they learned in working with the graduate course to "bring together theory, evidence and practice to enhance student learning and develop AIL assessment activities for the undergraduate course" (Adams et al. 2016). That experience led them to develop "self-guided formative online activities to provide consistent feedback to students, follow-up information and guidance related to assigned questions." Along with those assessments, the students took part in a follow-up tutorial "in which tutor and peers would provide feedback on the research questions, and where students would also have an opportunity to comment on others' submissions." In addition to the online components, campus-based students also received a face-to-face library workshop, and a website was provided "where students from both face to face and distance learning classes could ask questions and interact with one another." The most interesting part of this online component is that, while the comments and questions were monitored by librarians, staff "only responded if students were unable to assist each other or provided incorrect information." Thus while peer instruction was encouraged, librarians were able to step in and correct misconceptions or address gaps in knowledge in a timely fashion. Including all of these elements provided the librarians with rich assessment data and the students with an enhanced learning environment, since they received consistent feedback and guidance and were also encouraged to synthesize their learning to answer questions or to provide meaningful comments on their fellow students' work.

Peer teaching has also been implemented within the context of one-shot library instruction. Librarians at the University of Maryland, College Park, used a flipped classroom model to provide library instruction, designing information literacy modules within the university's course management system that students completed before the face-to-face session. A week prior to library instruction, students were enrolled in the library course within the learning management system and "working as a team, students were assigned a specific module in advance of class to present to their peers" (Carroll, Tchangalova, and Harrington 2016). During class, "students led the sessions as peer educators, delivering their brief presentations, while the librarians acted as facilitators" and their peers, using a rubric developed by the librarians, scored each other's presentations. In this case, each team of students was tasked with learning about a key information literacy concept outside of class and then instructed their fellow students on that concept during the one-shot session. In addition, students provided evaluative feedback on each team's presentation, "enabling students to reach higher levels of Bloom's taxonomy, a commonly used framework to assess student learning," while also "reinforcing the topics addressed in the module." This use of the flipped classroom model allowed librarians to engage students in a meaningful way during a one-shot session, activate higher-order thinking skills, and act more as guides on the side while students both taught and evaluated each other.

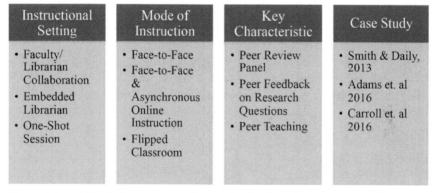

Instructional Setting	Mode of Instruction	Key Characteristic	Case Study
• Faculty/ Librarian Collaboration • Embedded Librarian • One-Shot Session	• Face-to-Face • Face-to-Face & Asynchronous Online Instruction • Flipped Classroom	• Peer Review Panel • Peer Feedback on Research Questions • Peer Teaching	• Smith & Daily, 2013 • Adams et. al 2016 • Carroll et. al 2016

Figure 4.4. Method of assessment: Peer evaluation/peer instruction. Jennifer S. Ferguson.

Performative Task-Based Assignments

Performative task-based assignments and performance assessments are a common method of authentic assessment and have been implemented across a wide variety of settings, both online and face-to-face, including in credit-bearing information literacy courses, embedded librarianship, tiered information literacy programs, and one-shot sessions. Because all modes of assessment are easier to implement when librarians have more time with students, whether throughout the semester or for two or more classes, this section will concentrate on cases in which performative task-based assignments were used within the one-shot setting. For example, librarians at Saint Leo University used a flipped classroom model to enhance information literacy instruction in a synchronous online environment. In collaboration with faculty, librarians developed learning outcomes and instructional materials that students would complete prior to the online library instruction session. Because the materials were developed in collaboration with faculty, the "instructor and librarian endeavored to create a clear connection between the relevance of the required information literacy activities and subsequent assignments" (Hawes and Adamson 2016), which as we have seen motivates students to complete tasks in a more intentional manner. In this case, the librarian developed "a series of worksheets that added the authentic task component" to the learning activities included in the asynchronous modules, which reinforced the learning outcomes and provided the teaching librarian with "the opportunity to catch any misunderstandings about the process in her feedback." This method allowed the librarian not only to employ an authentic task-based assessment but also to provide the kind of timely feedback that helps close the loop and reinforce student learning. The instruction librarian in this case grades the worksheets and provides a written summary to the class regarding the skills they need to demonstrate. In addition, this summary "provides the instructor and librarian with feedback upon which to redesign and re-craft sections of the modules where students consistently have had trouble."

Because students were required to complete several asynchronous modules prior to a one-shot synchronous instruction session, the librarians at Saint Leo were able to employ several task-based assignments during the course of the semester. However, most librarians who teach one-shot sessions in any context rarely have that luxury. Nevertheless, despite the well-known limitations of traditional one-shot sessions, task-based assignments can be incorporated into that instructional setting. For example, librarians at the University of North Carolina at Greensboro collaborated with the communications studies department not only to authentically assess information literacy skills but also to use those assessments to revise instructional practices and improve student learning. In this case, students had time to search for material on their topics and begin to complete a worksheet-based performance evaluation during a seventy-five-minute one-shot library instruction session. The worksheets were directly related to a communications theory–based assignment that students needed to complete in an upper-level communications course. The worksheets asked "students to define their theory and application and then choose books and articles related to their paper topic" (Natalle and Crowe 2013). This type of assignment requires students to exercise higher-order skills not only to find appropriate materials but also to demonstrate how they might apply a specific theory. The worksheets were due one week after instruction and the librarians used a rubric to evaluate them, assessing "whether the articles are from appropriate journals, are primary sources, and if they include both the theory and the context." After the instruction librarian evaluated the worksheets, they were sent to the professor for "further comments and grading before being returned to the students." This type of faculty-librarian collaboration on assessment both emphasizes the importance of information literacy and also directly connects library instruction with discipline-specific course learning outcomes, making it more relevant to students and promoting knowledge transfer. In addition to connecting library learning to discipline-specific learning, "this authentic assessment of an assignment that was part of the sequence of the course provided evidence that students were not acquiring the skills that both the teaching faculty and librarians wanted them to learn." Thus, they revised the pedagogy to improve student performance, and that adjustment "resulted in higher performance scores for student learning objectives involving research skills." In addition, this method of authentic assessment helped motivate the communication studies department to "emphasize and assess information literacy skills in all courses." In this case, authentic assessment resulted in stronger faculty-library collaboration, improved student learning, and supplied evidence that information literacy skills are crucial to student success in completing their coursework.

As we have seen, though, that type of strong collaboration between teaching faculty and librarians is not always possible, and some faculty members doubt librarians' preparation to be teachers. However, librarians can still develop and implement authentic task-based assignments for information literacy instruction. For example, librarians at Ball State University provide instruction in one of the most common settings in which it occurs, which is within one-shot course-integrated sessions in the first-year writing program, with library instructors teaching a large number of sessions for courses that include consistent content across sections. In this case, librarians had the ability to employ any one of a number of different formative assessments in order to compare results across sections, but the most common form of assessment was a task-based worksheet that measured learning outcomes such as identifying keywords and generating search strategies, identifying library resources or databases, and evaluating information sources (Jarrell 2014). One of the most interesting aspects of this method is that "in addition to measuring student understanding of these concepts in information literacy sessions, this plan allowed us to see which information literacy concepts were being taught by our faculty partners and requested as part of the information literacy sessions." Comparing those concepts across sections allowed the librarians to understand "what skills and concepts were being emphasized by our faculty and assessed as part of their writing courses," which helps librarians develop authentic tasks that are "meaningful and connected to real assignments and course learning goals." Thus, while there was more limited faculty-librarian collaboration, the librarians were able to gain a greater understanding of faculty needs by comparing outcomes and assessments across sections. In addition, the assessment results also demonstrated the need for librarians to "reduce the number of 'essential' topics to be covered in sessions." Instead, it was deemed more valuable for librarians to provide in-depth instruction on the "most important one or two concepts," and planning for instruction "focused on information literacy concepts rather than point and click instruction," which resulted in a more productive use of the limited time available in a one-shot session. In this case, the librarians were able to use authentic formative assessment techniques to improve student learning, develop learning outcomes more closely tied to class assignments, and make better use of their limited time with students.

In all of these cases, a key component of successfully implementing task-based assignments was to develop information literacy learning outcomes closely tied to course learning outcomes, which increases the material's relevancy to the students and encourages knowledge transfer. This shared understanding of learning outcomes—whether developed through direct collaboration with faculty or by comparing information across sections of the same course, also helps librarians create more authentic assessment instruments. For example, librarians at Virginia Commonwealth University working with a sophomore-level research and writing course developed library learning outcomes for this course that were "mapped to the learning outcomes mutually agreed upon between librarians and UNIV 200 faculty" (Gariepy, Stout, and Hodge 2016). Based on those learning outcomes, the librarians developed a worksheet that prompted students to perform several tasks, including writing out their research question, identifying the most important concepts in that question, developing search terms, and finding relevant scholarly material. Similar to the Ball State case, librarians at Virginia Commonwealth "had flexibility in their pedagogical approach to help students achieve the learning outcomes associated with each session." This flexibility is especially important when several instruction librarians are working with a large number of sections of the same course. Because teaching librarians, just like faculty, have a wide array of teaching styles, most of which are effective but all of which are different, developing standardized learning outcomes and standard task-based assignments tied to course learning outcomes can help ensure that students in each section learn what they need to know to succeed in that course. In addition, standardized assignments also make it possible for librarians to develop scoring rubrics, that allow them to assess student performance more equitably across sections. These performance assessments can also help librarians understand which pedagogical approaches work better than others in order to improve their own teaching practice. Interestingly, at Virginia Commonwealth librarians also "had flexibility in when and how they asked students to complete the worksheet." While most students completed the worksheet during the one-shot instruction session, some librarians had students watch video tutorials before class, complete the worksheet, and bring it with them to class—much like the flipped classroom model. In this case, in order to add more authenticity, the worksheets were designed as both an assessment and a learning tool and were returned promptly to the students. This type of instructional flexibility is especially interesting in light of the standardized assignment and scoring rubric and can provide direct evidence of the effectiveness of a particular instructional method. While the librarians at Virginia Commonwealth did not analyze the assessment results in this way, they did find, much like the librarians at Ball State, that students who had more time for hands-on practice performed better and that paring down the number of concepts taught in a one-shot session led to improved student learning. Thus, they used the assessment results to streamline "the instruction portion of the class to provide students with additional search time" and to improve and modify their "personal teaching practices as well as our instruction program."

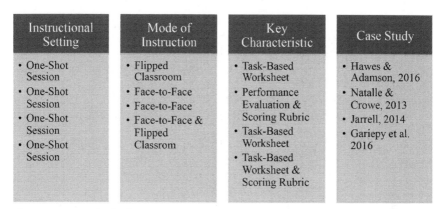

Instructional Setting	Mode of Instruction	Key Characteristic	Case Study
• One-Shot Session • One-Shot Session • One-Shot Session • One-Shot Session	• Flipped Classroom • Face-to-Face • Face-to-Face • Face-to-Face & Flipped Classrom	• Task-Based Worksheet • Performance Evaluation & Scoring Rubric • Task-Based Worksheet • Task-Based Worksheet & Scoring Rubric	• Hawes & Adamson, 2016 • Natalle & Crowe, 2013 • Jarrell, 2014 • Gariepy et al. 2016

Figure 4.5. Method of assessment: Performative task-based assignments. Jennifer S. Ferguson.

Problem-Based Activities

Problem-based activities are similar to performative task-based assignments in that they require students to analyze, synthesize, and apply what they have learned in order to complete a particular task. However, problem-based activities generally focus on "real-world" as opposed to academic tasks. In order for students to write effective college-level research papers, they need to master specific research skills such as how to search library databases, identify appropriate scholarly information, and use that information to construct an argument. Task-based assignments are well suited to assess this type of academic competency. Nevertheless, some disciplines also require their students to master information skills that will be essential to succeed in particular work environments after they have graduated. For example, upper-level students majoring in journalism have different information needs than upper-level students majoring in nursing. While both sets of students will need to learn how to access and evaluate information in order to do their jobs well, the types of information competencies that employers will expect them to have differ greatly. However, in both cases, they will need to use information to solve a problem, and problem-based activities can provide authentic assessment of the types of information literacy skills these students require. For example, noting that "adult learners are more capable of absorbing skills or lessons through problem-based or task-centered exercises" (Halpern and Tucker 2015), librarians at the University of Southern California (USC) developed an online "information literacy toolkit" for social work and journalism students with those needs in mind. In this case, the librarians designed the tutorials to begin with a short story in order to help students "understand why a certain concept or set of skills is useful or necessary to them." The tutorials include scenarios such as "Knowing-Where-to-Look," in which "a fictional student spends hours looking for Department of Justice Statistics in a scholarly database because he does not realize those statistics can easily be found on the Department's Web site." These tutorials are placed in strategic spots on the library's website and completed at relevant points during the semester so that students encounter important skill sets at their point of need. For example, social work students "complete the Developing Keywords tutorial before the in-class library session, as they work on their first literature review assignment." In addition to telling stories that help students contextualize library instruction to make it more relevant to their needs, the librarians at USC designed their tutorials to focus on problem-based learning. Thus, "instead of lecturing to deliver content, the instructor sets up problems for students to solve, either independently or collaboratively." Each slide has very little explanatory text, which echoes what many librarians have found when they attempt to construct effective performative task-based assignments; the most effective modules involve minimal instruction of relatively few concepts followed by the performance of a specific task or the solving of an information problem. At USC, "students complete exercises, reflect on how those exercises develop a particular skill and receive feedback to reinforce those connections," which ensures that the exercises are both a learning tool and an authentic assessment.

The USC example also points to one of the additional strengths of problem-based activities: they can be scaled up for large classes. And while the flipped classroom model is probably most ideal for implementing this form of authentic assessment to a large class, since students complete the exercises outside of class and librarians can spend face-to-face class time correcting misperceptions and filling gaps in knowledge, problem-based activities have also been employed in face-to-face sessions for large lecture classes. Similar to the USC case in which problem-based activities are focused on disciplines like journalism and social work, business students also have particular information needs that can be addressed with problem-based activities. For example, librarians at the University of Houston have used the case method as a form of authentic problem-based learning and assessment. This method is particularly well suited to information literacy instruction for business classes since it is often a form of instruction familiar to students majoring in that subject. At the University of Houston, the case method was used with a large introductory business class; students were divided into groups and worked together to "define what the known parameters of a research problem are and what areas still need to be researched" (Martin 2015). While the research problem they are asked to solve does not represent an entire case, it echoes the types of problems that students will need to solve once they graduate and move into the workforce. These problems include questions such as: "Does the addition of the Marriott Marquis [hotel] to downtown Houston increase or decrease room occupancy rates at other downtown hotels? Explain what the known areas of the research problem are and what areas need to be further researched and how they might be researched." Working together, students attempt to answer one or more of the questions in the problem they have been assigned and then each group reports out on their solution. Once "as many groups as possible have participated, the librarian offers feedback on the answers and students are given the opportunity to ask any remaining questions." At Houston, this method was used in classes of up to three hundred students, and the librarians maintain that the method "remains the same whether the class is 60 students or 600 students," though larger classes often require two librarians to be present during instruction. In this case, librarians effectively used a problem-based activity as both a learning tool and an authentic assessment for very large classes. That said, they also found that providing meaningful feedback was not only one of the most important aspects of this assessment but also one of the most challenging to implement due to time limitations. Since students are particularly interested in discovering what they did wrong and how they can get it right next time, it makes "the debriefing portion of the assessment especially important." Indeed, as we have seen, providing meaningful feedback helps close the loop and reinforces the lessons students learned. To implement problem-based activities like this in large one-shot sessions, librarians need to remember to leave adequate time or to develop an alternative method for offering that feedback.

Embedded librarians have also employed problem-based activities over the course of multiple information literacy instruction sessions. For example, a librarian and a faculty member at Elmhurst College collaborated on the development of a problem-based learning approach for students in an introductory class in American government. In this case, students "were engaged in a group project in which they acted as media consultants for the political candidate of their choice" (Cook and Walsh 2012). The librarian provided two information literacy instruction sessions, one of which focused "on searching for and identifying appropriate sources" while the other focused "on evaluating sources, particularly in terms of credibility and bias." Both of these sessions were centered on solving the information problems students would encounter as media consultants, moving "beyond an informal discussion of choices to an explicit determination of what they need to know and how they will acquire that knowledge." In order to get at those concepts, the activity included components such as researching current events relevant to their candidates and political parties, identifying credible sources of information about those events, and recognizing bias in its many forms. Along with the practical value of solving "real world" problems relevant to political professionals, this "approach provides an opportunity for students to practice and examine the information literacy skills necessary to participatory democracy." The instructors administered a pre-/post-test in order to assess whether the students gained the necessary skills as they solved their information problems. In addition to a self-assessment component, the pre-/post-test included more authentic open-ended questions that asked students to apply what they had learned. In addition, the instructors also assigned a reflection paper that helped them "to gather student feedback on the strengths and weaknesses of the project." Not surprisingly, the instructors found that the self-assessment portion of the pre-/post-test was "insufficient to gauge actual ability" and that the open-ended questions in which students were required to apply what they had learned were far better measures of the learning that had taken place. Moreover, the instructors also found that the problem-based exercise "not only increased student sensitivity to the credibility and bias of

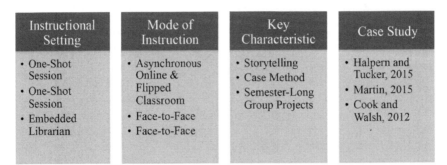

Instructional Setting	Mode of Instruction	Key Characteristic	Case Study
• One-Shot Session • One-Shot Session • Embedded Librarian	• Asynchronous Online & Flipped Classroom • Face-to-Face • Face-to-Face	• Storytelling • Case Method • Semester-Long Group Projects	• Halpern and Tucker, 2015 • Martin, 2015 • Cook and Walsh, 2012

Figure 4.6. Method of assessment: Problem-based activities. Jennifer S. Ferguson.

sources, but some students also reported a greater likelihood to use these skills to engage in politics." This kind of student reflection indicates that the problem-based activity resulted in the kind of knowledge transfer that is important not only to students while they are in college but also might promote lifelong learning.

Quizzes

While fixed-answer quizzes are generally not considered authentic assessments, librarians can design quizzes in a more authentic manner if they require students to synthesize and apply what they have learned. As we have seen, quizzes have many advantages in terms of design and scalability, especially when they measure only library learning outcomes and do not include other discipline-specific components. However, authentic quizzes do retain many of the advantages of fixed-answer quizzes, especially in the online environment, and have been implemented successfully in a number of places. For example, librarians at the University of California, Berkeley, have developed a number of innovative approaches to teaching and assessment based on the needs of the subject disciplines with which they work. In one case, a librarian working with a large introductory biology class discovered that the traditional fifty-minute one-shot session that included a graded homework assignment was no longer viable as the class time would no longer be available for library instruction and delays in returning the homework assignments failed to reinforce the intended learning outcomes. In response, information literacy instruction for this class was moved to the online environment, and students completed it outside of class time. Thus instead of attending one fifty-minute in-class session, students were asked to complete "six online learning modules consisting of instructional videos embedded in the LibGuides content management system. Each video was 35 minutes long and was accompanied by text summaries and helpful links" (Loo et al. 2016). While these online learning modules are a fairly typical mode of instruction, the librarian who designed these modules included less typical authentic assessments that students completed after engaging with each tutorial. These assessments "were delivered in multiple choice and short answer formats that added a higher-order problem-solving element to the assignment." Along with asking students to develop search strategies, the quizzes also required students to refine searches to retrieve specific results and to write citations. Most importantly, "instantaneous autograding of each question enabled efficient assessment and provided students with real-time feedback." Because the platform that was used for assignment delivery could accommodate "variations and minor errors in student responses," it was used to create and administer more authentic quizzes than can be employed using less functional software that allows only for multiple-choice and other fixed-answer options. Because of its scalability, this method thus retained one of the main strengths of quizzes as a mode of assessment; since autograding "became not only an efficient means to consistently grade more than 700 student assignments," it also provided an instrument for authentically assessing student learning. Because students were immediately tested on their learning and were presented with instant feedback on their answers, these quizzes functioned as both a learning tool and a measure of student learning. In addition, if a student's answer was incorrect they "could refer to embedded contextual help" and re-submit their answers, which "helped students learn from their mistakes" and "facilitated iterative learning for content mastery."

While librarians at the University of California, Berkeley, might perhaps have access to the kinds of tools that make constructing authentic quizzes within online tutorials more accessible, librarians have been able to implement them successfully in other settings. For example, librarians at the University of Wisconsin–Madison's engineering library designed a credit-bearing hybrid information literacy course in which quizzes represented 54 percent of a student's grade. Because they made up such a large proportion of graded work, the librarians had to design the quizzes to measure a variety of learning outcomes. In this case, the quizzes were administered online and ranged "from four to seven questions each, with a variety of question types (multiple choice, true-false, open-ended, among others)" (Wheeler, Vellardita, and Kindschi 2010). Since students were required to take a significant number of quizzes, many, such as the true-false and multiple-choice options, were not designed as authentic assessments. However, two types of quizzes included authentic components such as short answers and, most interestingly, task-based assignments. The librarians designed some quizzes in which students were given "an information task to complete, and may include a link out to a database that must be searched to find the correct answer." In addition, students had "one hour for each quiz attempt, and they may take a quiz up to three times to obtain the highest score." While the librarians in this case used quizzes as one mode of assessment in a credit-bearing course, this type of authentic online quiz can be adapted to a number of instructional settings such as the flipped classroom model in which students would complete an online module prior to a one-shot session, or within standalone information literacy tutorial modules. The components of this type of quiz that make it an authentic assessment include requiring students to synthesize their knowledge in order to apply it to completing a task as well as the immediate feedback students received. Because they were allowed to re-take the quiz up to three times, these quizzes also facilitated the kind of iterative learning that promotes "content mastery."

Although both of the prior examples employ authentic quizzes within the online environment, authentic quizzes have also been administered in face-to-face one-shot sessions. For example, librarians at Colorado State University–Pueblo initially designed a paper-based assessment that students completed at the end of a library instruction session. In this case, "students were given evaluations consisting of three to five open-ended, short-answer questions" (Seeber 2013). In order to ensure that students thoroughly and thoughtfully completed the assessments, the paper forms were branded as library quizzes and students were required to include their name on them. Even though these quizzes had no bearing on their course grades, simply branding them as quizzes and requiring students to include their name "led to more thorough responses from students and higher response rates." The paper-based quizzes were subsequently migrated to an online form but retained their authentic components, continued to be administered at the end of a one-shot session, and included questions that prompted students to exercise higher-order thinking skills. For example, one question asks students to differentiate between the results and discussion sections of a scholarly article and explain how they differ. The librarians scored the quizzes using a rubric, and assessment results were shared with teaching faculty in order to help them better understand both their students' information literacy skill levels and the nature of information literacy learning outcomes. The Colorado State librarians found that this kind of sharing of assessment results had several benefits, including "a marked increase in IL sessions taking place," and suggest that "the seriousness with which the University Library is taking assessment and improvements to instruction" accounts for part of that increase. In addition, sharing a "quantitative analysis of student performance demonstrates to faculty that the library is making progress toward its student learning goals and improving research skills on campus." In this case, systematic assessment using authentic quizzes helped the librarians achieve two goals—to improve student learning and to report out to key stakeholders in order to demonstrate the library's value. As we have seen, the ability to report out significant assessment data, whether through sharing it with faculty or with higher administration, is increasingly important for libraries to do in order to make evident their contributions to institutional goals. Authentic assessment allows librarians to gather and share significant information about what is increasingly becoming a key institutional learning outcome.

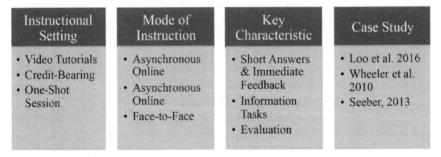

Instructional Setting	Mode of Instruction	Key Characteristic	Case Study
• Video Tutorials • Credit-Bearing • One-Shot Session	• Asynchronous Online • Asynchronous Online • Face-to-Face	• Short Answers & Immediate Feedback • Information Tasks • Evaluation	• Loo et al. 2016 • Wheeler et al. 2010 • Seeber, 2013

Figure 4.7. Method of assessment: Quizzes. Jennifer S. Ferguson.

Reflections

Reflections that prompt students to analyze and synthesize their own learning can be a powerful form of authentic assessment, since reflections encourage students to answer their own why questions. In addition, reflections that use guided questions can be an especially useful mode of assessment. For example, librarians at the University of California, Merced, implemented a six-question reflection as one mode of assessment in course-integrated instruction for a first-year writing course. Codesigned with writing faculty, this course was structured so that faculty introduced students "to content about the research process and information literacy via activities, readings, tutorials, and reflections before students had in-person instruction with a librarian" (Squibb and Mikkelsen 2016). In this case, the librarians reinforced content taught by the writing faculty, which encouraged students to think of the writing and research process as inextricably entwined, after which the librarians administered the final six-question reflection. Once students completed the reflections, the librarians scored them using a rubric. The six questions that guided students through the reflection not only asked students to reflect on specific tasks and processes, such as evaluating and selecting resources, developing research strategies, and transferring skills, but also prompted them to be specific and give examples. This type of reflection prompts students to examine their own processes and exercise higher-order thinking skills. It also helps students reinforce their own learning, enabling them to consider how and why their research processes and skills may have changed during the course of the semester. After implementing this revised information literacy curriculum, the librarians felt that the "student reflections provided the team with insight into students' struggles and successes during Writing 10 as they strove to develop as researchers who could successfully work with evidence." However, and quite interestingly, they also found that their decision to use scoring rubrics "tended to mask the richness of the evidence—what students were thinking, attempting, and changing as they researched." This problem tended to manifest itself in the differences between students who scored in the "Advanced" and "Developing" ranges. Based on the rubric, students who scored in the Advanced range "expressed the type of thinking and research practices team members hoped to see," but "students who scored in the Developing range still wrote statements indicating that they too had made progress in developing the knowledge, skills, and attitudes of student researchers." The rubric's inability to capture this kind of nuance points to one of the limitations of scoring rubrics. As we have seen, rubrics can often be difficult to implement because of issues with standardization and inter-grader reliability. In this case, the rubric was also a bit too rigid to use as a grading tool for student reflections. While the librarians found that the reflections were a valuable form of assessment, in the future they "would plan to code the students' text as a preferred form of analysis over a rubric." Finally, in this case the librarians also presented their assessment findings to outside stakeholders from the university's faculty and administration who "seemed most interested in this assessment when we have highlighted student statements from their reflective writing that suggest growth in students' research attitudes and behaviors." This response indicates the value of this type of authentic assessment not just for student learning but also for reporting out to institutional stakeholders.

Librarians at The College of New Jersey (TCNJ) were also able to implement student reflections as a mode of assessment for innovative one-shot sessions that included a hands-on Wikipedia editing exercise as part of a larger lesson on library research. In this case, students were prompted to reflect on Wikipedia during a "facilitated class discussion before the hands-on Wikipedia editing activity" (Oliver 2015). This class discussion "began with a think-pair-share exercise that asked students to reflect on Wikipedia's usefulness and on its limitations." The librarians started the discussion by asking guiding questions, after which the students reflected on the question individually and then jotted "down one idea or concept per sticky note." After reflecting individually, students exchanged their ideas with a classmate, then with the rest of the class and the instructor, and finally "the sticky notes were collected and analyzed." This use of student reflections within a think-pair-share activity is especially interesting because the sticky notes provided librarians with a kind of qualitative pre-test, which helped them understand how and what students were thinking prior to a hands-on exercise. After the hands-on Wikipedia editing exercise, librarians were also able to observe "the extent to which students completed the Wikipedia-editing tasks," that provided them with an additional task-based assessment. The students were also asked to respond to questions on an exit survey, most of which "were free-field and open ended, so students could provide more than one answer," much like minute papers, which provided the librarians with an additional form of authentic assessment, all within the context of a two-hour one-shot session. The TCNJ librarians found the student reflections to be a very useful tool and going forward would recommend that they are used to assess "a wider range of student skills, attitudes and behaviors, thus allowing more robust post-intervention analysis of the effect these activities have on learning." This conclusion underscores the importance of employing multiple forms of assessment whenever possible, since they measure different aspects of student learning. For example, the TCNJ librarians used student reflections as a kind of pre-test to help them understand the students' prior knowledge about Wikipedia, had the students perform a particular task, and then asked the students to answer guided questions about what they learned after completing the task, thus closing the assessment loop. However, since both the pre- and post-test instruments focused on a relatively narrow Wikipedia-editing exercise, the librarians were unable to assess what students learned during the traditional library instruction portion of the class and whether the Wikipedia exercise encouraged other kinds of learning. Nevertheless, this example demonstrates how multiple short authentic assessments can be integrated into a one-shot session in order both to promote and measure student learning.

While reflections have been successfully implemented in one-shot sessions, they are most commonly used in credit-bearing courses, both face-to-face and online, where librarians have the ability to assess student learning using a wide variety of instruments. However, although they are relatively common in credit-bearing courses, reflective writing has been used more intentionally in some settings than in others. For example, instructors in the iSchool at the University of Sheffield used reflective writing as a key form of assessment within a credit-bearing business intelligence module for undergraduate students. In this case, the instructors combined problem-based activities, peer evaluation, and reflective writing, with students working "as business intelligence consultants on behalf of real businesses, carrying out business research for the company" (Sen and McKinney 2014). This problem-based activity helped students "gain a deeper understanding of the need for information in a business context." Throughout the module, information literacy skills are reinforced as students begin to gain the "ability to react to business intelligence situations" as well as to adapt their information-seeking and evaluation strategies in order to respond to specific conditions. While the instructors designed the module to help students develop information literacy competencies, they also wanted to "find a way of assessing this development" and designed a workshop activity in which "students are asked to write a short reflection using a template provided and then peer review each others' work." This type of reflection not only encourages students to evaluate their own skills and abilities but also includes the type of peer evaluation that "places them in the position of the assessor." As we have seen, this type of peer teaching encourages students to engage in higher-order thinking in order to help each other "identify strategies they could both use to deepen the level of reflection." The reflections that students completed during the workshop were not assessed, but instead they provided the foundation for students to submit a longer piece of reflective writing that was included with their graded work at the end of the module. In this case, the instructors intended the activity to "practice, and develop their reflective writing skills in a supportive environment and be able to make mistakes in a non-assessed environment." For librarians teaching credit-bearing courses that focus on information literacy, this method

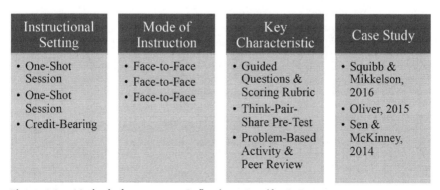

Instructional Setting	Mode of Instruction	Key Characteristic	Case Study
• One-Shot Session	• Face-to-Face	• Guided Questions & Scoring Rubric	• Squibb & Mikkelson, 2016
• One-Shot Session	• Face-to-Face	• Think-Pair-Share Pre-Test	• Oliver, 2015
• Credit-Bearing	• Face-to-Face	• Problem-Based Activity & Peer Review	• Sen & McKinney, 2014

Figure 4.8. Method of assessment: Reflections. Jennifer S. Ferguson.

provides a particularly interesting example in that it combines multiple authentic assessments in which learning outcomes and their measurement are closely related. The problem-based teaching approach helps students understand how information literacy competencies are important in "real-world" situations, while the reflective writing reinforces students' ability to think critically about their own and other students' learning.

SUMMATIVE ASSESSMENT

Annotated Bibliographies

Annotated bibliographies are a frequently employed summative assessment in credit-bearing courses, tiered information literacy programs, and embedded librarianship. Given the difficulties inherent in directly correlating the effects of one-shot library instruction on student coursework, this section will focus on some of the exemplary uses of annotated bibliographies in other instructional settings. For example, at California State University Channel Islands (CI), information literacy has been adopted as a general education requirement. The library provides information literacy in a tiered program where "the library's IL Coordinator targets specific first-year (freshman), third-year (upper division) and fourth-year (capstone) courses for library instruction each semester" (Hoffman and LaBonte 2012). However, as a newly founded campus the librarians at CI had no access to any prior information literacy assessment data, which offered them both a challenge and an opportunity. In response, librarians collaborated with first-year writing faculty to develop an authentic assessment of student work, with the intent to "create a rubric that could be applied to all first-year writing assignments that require research" and eventually to develop an instrument that could be used to assess student work in each year of the IL program. In this case, the librarians discovered that the rubric was not necessarily simple to develop and systematically apply for many of the same reasons discussed earlier. However, they did find that "the reflective component of the annotated bibliography greatly facilitated the rating process," because "raters were better able to see evidence of a student's intent in choosing or incorporating a source into an assignment, even if that intent wasn't immediately clear from examining the assignment alone." Because CI's annotated bibliography assignment required "students to reflect upon the research assignment at hand, locate what they consider to be appropriate resources and then reflect upon each of these sources individually," it combined a task-based assessment with a reflection. In this case, the number of first-year library instruction sessions varied from section to section, which meant that students received different levels of information literacy instruction, from a one-shot session to multiple classes with a librarian. Thus, the design of the annotated bibliography to include a reflection component was extremely important in order to "highlight the research process undertaken by students and to discern the reasoning behind why students chose and incorporated the sources that they did." This reflective annotated bibliography thus helped librarians overcome some of the limitations of student bibliographies as information literacy assessment instruments. Moreover, since the annotated bibliography was the precursor to a larger research assignment, it was both highly relevant to the students and "helped raters better identify evidence of IL in students' written work." Most importantly, close faculty-librarian collaboration on designing and assessing an authentic assignment helped instruction librarians overcome some of the well-known difficulties in correlating one-shot sessions with the evidence of information literacy proficiency in student coursework.

Embedded librarians have also been successful in using annotated bibliographies as authentic summative assessments. For example, embedded librarians at Queensborough Community College (QCC) used a scaffolded instruction strategy in which "three library sessions were offered to each section of the English 101 or 102 classes throughout the semester," and each class was "designed to provide students with step by step instructions so they were able to incorporate what they learned into their research papers at their own pace" (Kim and Dolan 2015). While faculty assigned the research papers, the librarians required students "to submit an annotated bibliography after the third library session." The annotated bibliography required students to cite a minimum of three sources and counted as five points of their final grade. The instruction librarians used a five-point rubric to score the bibliographies, which they designed specifically for the type of beginning students typical at QCC and emphasized concepts such as evaluating the credibility of sources and students' ability to summarize them. In addition, "students were encouraged to include quotations in the summary as a method to ensure that they read the articles for the research paper." This use of annotated bibliographies is particularly interesting because it addresses the needs of beginning students, many of whom are not necessarily native English speakers. Annotated bibliographies are most often employed as summative assessments for research-based courses or capstone projects. However, in this case, librarians assigned a relatively short annotated bibliography as a learning artifact for students who are at the very outset of their careers in higher education, which makes possible authentic summative assessment of information literacy for first-year students. In the end, the librarians at QCC found that "a vast majority of students demonstrated that they conducted research in library databases, chose reliable sources from scholarly journals, and performed proper evaluations when they selected Web resources." The only real difficulty students had in completing the annotated bibliography assignment was with proper citation format, despite having one of the three sessions devoted to citation—which points to a basic conundrum about what information literacy instruction should ideally encompass. Given the time limitations inherent in most instructional settings, citation style—whether MLA, APA, Chicago, or any other—might more legitimately be considered an area better addressed by faculty or the campus writing center. As the librarians at QCC note, "It would not have been possible to focus so closely on citations if the students had not attended an embedded librarian program with three sessions," and even with the luxury of a session focused solely on citation, students still had trouble comprehending "basic citation rules." This finding reinforces the discussion around the limitations of authentic assessment for diverse populations when the only assessment instrument is a writing artifact. In addition, it highlights two important considerations in terms of designing learning outcomes and instruments to measure them. First, librarians need to think about the most important concepts that students need to learn in order to become better users of information and ask themselves questions about how best to address and assess them. For example, is citation style as important as evaluation? How much time do you have to teach the concepts students need to learn? Can you collaborate with faculty or with the campus writing center to teach the mechanics of citation style and focus on more important overarching information literacy concepts? These questions can lead not only to better teaching and learning but also to more authentic information literacy assessment.

Along with their usefulness for summative assessment of the information literacy competencies of first-year students, annotated bibliographies have also been employed in assessing adult learners. Librarians at Duquesne University often work with nontraditional working adult students enrolled as undergraduates in the School for Leadership and Professional Advancement, and in response the program "offers several required courses that emphasize transitional skills for success in higher education and careers" (Rapchak, Lewis, et al. 2015). These students "are required to take a separate IL course—a three-credit, 8-week course, taught face to face or online by library faculty" that focuses on many critical information literacy competencies, including "using the university's databases and catalog, evaluating information, and understanding issues of plagiarism and copyright infringement." In this case, the librarians designed an annotated bibliography assignment to provide a summative assessment of course learning outcomes and then designed a rubric in order to score them. The annotated bibliography was the capstone assignment for the course and was similar across sections and instructors. Each assignment required students to use the "research tools introduced in the course . . . to find appropriate resources on a research topic. Students were to cite these resources, summarize them, and provide an annotation." Because this was a credit-bearing course and librarians had the time to teach a number of concepts, the assignment asked students to address multiple criteria, such as currency, authority, and accuracy, as well as how those criteria related to their research questions. Interestingly, unlike the QCC students who mainly struggled with citation style, the nontraditional students at Duquesne "struggled most with evaluation" and did not "adequately support their analyses and/or had a variety of missing evaluation criteria." Since this assignment was the capstone for a credit-bearing course, the level of sophistication necessary to evaluate more than three sources, even with multiple instruction sessions, might have proved more of a challenge for nontraditional students—especially adult students—than initially expected. Based on this result, the Duquesne librarians maintain that "instructors should not assume that nontraditional students have IL skills" and "graduates must learn their options for accessing quality information using available resources." This result reinforces the need for increased teaching of "soft skills" such as evaluation rather than the more mechanistic point-and-click abilities. After receiving library instruction students may be able to search a database, but they still might have a very hard time sorting out good information from bad, no matter its origin. In addition, they continue to struggle with incorporating appropriate sources into their writing assignments, which once again points to the need for course instructors "to address IL skills in their courses with practice and feedback opportunities" in order to "allow students to understand the depth of critical thinking required to understand and analyze a source." As information sources proliferate across platforms—from curated library databases to the wild and woolly web environment, information literacy instruction that addresses increasingly crucial skills and abilities is more important than ever. In addition, authentic assessment that can help both librarians and faculty to measure whether or not students have mastered those skills and abilities is essential to assuring that students are able to function in the wider information universe once they graduate. The Duquesne example reinforces the necessity for faculty and librarians to collaborate on teaching and assessing what has become not only an essential skill for success at school but also for students to be able to transfer these important skills in order to function effectively at work and in society as a whole. This "real-world" component is the essence of authentic assessment and applies to all students, both traditional undergraduates and nontraditional adult learners.

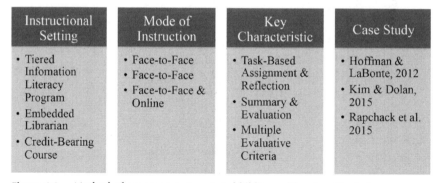

Instructional Setting	Mode of Instruction	Key Characteristic	Case Study
• Tiered Infomation Literacy Program • Embedded Librarian • Credit-Bearing Course	• Face-to-Face • Face-to-Face • Face-to-Face & Online	• Task-Based Assignment & Reflection • Summary & Evaluation • Multiple Evaluative Criteria	• Hoffman & LaBonte, 2012 • Kim & Dolan, 2015 • Rapchack et al. 2015

Figure 4.9. Method of assessment: Annotated bibliographies. Jennifer S. Ferguson.

Portfolios

Similar to annotated bibliographies, librarians use portfolios for assessment most often in settings such as credit-bearing courses and embedded librarianship where librarians provide students with more than one instruction session during the course of a semester or throughout the course of a tiered information literacy program. Since portfolios contain multiple learning artifacts, from short written work and quizzes to longer research papers, they are generally not available as a summative assessment instrument for one-shot sessions. However, they have been constructively employed in both the face-to-face and online environments for longer form instruction. For example, librarians at the University of Connecticut used research portfolios to both teach and assess information literacy in a credit-bearing course. In this case, the librarians decided to implement authentic assessment as they "were interested in assessing students' multiple efforts at formulating a research problem, translating it into a focused topic, applying new search strategies, and analyzing and evaluating search results based on newly discovered knowledge and our feedback" (Sharma 2007). To achieve those assessment goals, the Connecticut librarians decided to collect student-learning artifacts in a web-based research portfolio through which they could concretely assess each of the skills they hoped students would acquire during the course. In addition, the choice of which artifacts to include also meant that the portfolios were "used both for teaching the research process and for collecting evidence to show that student learning has taken place." Each task that students were expected to master could be scaffolded in the portfolio so that students received feedback on each step in the research process, were encouraged to revise their work, and were taught to think critically as they reflected on their progress. This portfolio included eight samples of student work, including a statement of topic, a concept map, a research question, a research log, a research strategy, a selection of online sources, an annotated bibliography, and a final reflection. The students then uploaded their portfolios to the learning management system and shared their work with the rest of the class by creating individual web pages "with links to all sections of the portfolio." The Connecticut librarians developed a grading worksheet that included their criteria for evaluation of each section of the portfolio and distributed it to students "in advance so that they had a clear understanding of desired outcomes." In this case, the portfolio was designed to include all the elements of authentic assessment, as it required students to analyze, synthesize, and apply what they had learned, as well as offering students meaningful and consistent feedback that encouraged them to think critically. Moreover, the librarians also found that employing an authentic assessment instrument "validated a widely held notion that while students may perform quite well on typical tests with multiple-choice questions," that type of assessment only measures students' short-term ability to recall basic concepts. They go on to conclude that "such results could be misleading as they do not necessarily mean students can actually apply those skills and knowledge to real problems that require critical thinking."

Librarians have also used portfolios to assess specific learning outcomes in targeted credit-bearing courses. For example, librarians at Penn State University teach a library studies course on research methods to students preparing their honors theses. In this class, students are assigned tasks such as establishing a research problem; defining a topic; selecting resources; identifying search vocabularies; developing search statements and strategies; database searching; evaluating sources; and preparing literature reviews and annotated bibliographies using all material formats. In this case, the librarians found that the portfolios solved some of the problems with both learning and assessment that they had discovered in prior course iterations. For example, students perceived that the earlier version of the course "was fragmented and lacked coherence" and "there was little perceived connection between the assignment and its application to their thesis work, and no understanding of relatedness of each individual part building toward a whole" (Snavely and Wright 2003). To solve those problems, the Penn State librarians decided to employ portfolios to more authentically assess student learning as well as to help students understand how each individual piece built toward the final project rather than regarding "them as discrete entities" instead of "elements of a culminating project." Thus, the portfolio could be seen as a template for "the present and future information gathering aspects of their research," adding to the "real-world" nature of their learning. As with most portfolios, the librarians in this case gathered a variety of learning artifacts in order to measure student progress over time. However, they also went one step further in terms of using them to re-inforce student learning in a very concrete way. The Penn State research portfolio had two separate phases, with the first consisting of "the initial accumulation of assignments and activities that represent the evolution of the information gathering process." However, most interesting is the second phase of the portfolio, which was the "revised portfolio, where students were able to re-execute each assignment." In this case, "revising each of the assignments allowed both students and instructors to be reflective about the learning that had occurred, and provided students with a framework to support continued thesis research." Essentially this class required students to create two parallel portfolios, one of which included all of their original work, and the second of which included revised versions of each assignment along with faculty comments and students' notes, with the final result "a complete package that traced the development of their research" and provided them with a base on which to build their future work. This particular use of port-folios for assessment helped students connect library instruction to their needs in a more authentic way and encouraged them to think more critically about their own process and reflect and build on their learning. Thus, the portfolio acted as both a learning object and assessment instrument, providing the students with a deeper understanding of the research process and the librarians with a powerful method to assess student learning over time.

Portfolios have also been used to assess the information literacy competencies of adult learners and nontraditional students. Librarians at Teesside University teach a compulsory credit-bearing information literacy module to students en-rolled in the Negotiated Learning Scheme, which is a program that "was specifi-cally designed to attract adult learners who would not normally engage in higher education" (Sonley et al. 2007). In this case, the librarians turned to portfolios as an assessment that was both summative and developmental, which could demonstrate student progress over time and provide some measure of their skills and abilities at the end of the module. This approach was especially important since "adult learners are likely to be highly motivated to learn when they can see personal relevance" and "are more interested in practical application than theoretical issues." Thus, the module was designed so that it took "an experiential problem solving approach" and assessed students using a portfolio that gathered a number of learning artifacts that allowed "students to record activity, show progress and aid reflection" to provide them with scaffolded instruction and offer the librarians a more authentic assessment of student progress. For example, the portfolio included "three elements: a bibliography, evidence of the search processes and revisions, and a critical reflection on the process with an evaluation of the various sources used." In addition, students were given templates in order to provide them with a guided structure that helped them complete each artifact. Since the students in this program were nontraditional and not as prepared for university-level work as more traditional students, this kind of structure allowed the librarians to provide a clear set of expectations for what successful completion of each assignment would entail. Because the instructors understood "that part of their teaching would need to focus on making expectations as clear as possible so that students' performances really did reflect their capabilities," they also developed a handbook for the information literacy module that explained the purpose of the portfolio and provided clear assessment criteria. The template and the handbook helped take "away the anxiety about what was expected" and "gave them time to concentrate on what was really important." In the end, the Teesside librarians found that this type of portfolio assessment had significant benefits, including a better ability to identify "group misunderstandings or problems in grasping concepts," which can help facilitate better teaching going forward. Thus, in this case the portfolios served a dual purpose—providing a summative assessment of student learning as well as a formative assessment of the instructors' teaching. Because this type of dual assessment provides librarians with rich data on both teaching and learning, it can also be used to demonstrate value to outside stakeholders. For example, librarians can

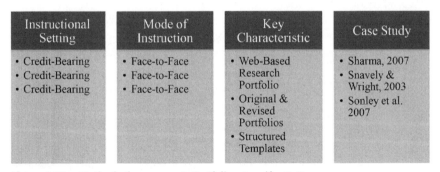

Instructional Setting	Mode of Instruction	Key Characteristic	Case Study
• Credit-Bearing • Credit-Bearing • Credit-Bearing	• Face-to-Face • Face-to-Face • Face-to-Face	• Web-Based Research Portfolio • Original & Revised Portfolios • Structured Templates	• Sharma, 2007 • Snavely & Wright, 2003 • Sonley et al. 2007

Figure 4.10. Method of assessment: Portfolios. Jennifer S. Ferguson.

communicate a culture of assessment to higher administration by demonstrating how they use authentic assessment data to inform better teaching strategies that have a positive impact on students' performance of critical competencies.

Pre-/Post-Tests

While time limitations can appear to be a daunting impediment to administering pre-/post-tests during a one-shot session, they have been successfully implemented in that setting within course-integrated library instruction. For example, a librarian and a faculty member at California State University, Long Beach, collaborated on a pre-/post-test assessment for students enrolled in an upper-division journalism course. In this case, they codesigned an assessment that measured both key news gathering and writing skills as well as information literacy competencies, adapting a "well-honed information gathering assignment" into a "mid-curriculum assessment of four of the five student-learning outcomes involving information gathering" (Brown and Kingsley-Wilson 2010). While the faculty member taught the course, the librarian provided one ninety-minute problem-based instruction session toward the middle of the semester that focused on finding background information, identifying experts, and locating basic statistical sources. In addition to locating information, students were also encouraged to critically evaluate what they found, which is a learning outcome essential for both information literacy and journalism, since an "'authentic' assessment of reporting skills would require that students demonstrate the ability to identify the six questions fundamental to reporting: who, what, when, where, why and how." In order to test journalism students in "as realistic a manner as possible" they designed a pre-/post-test to determine what students knew at the beginning of the course and compare those initial results to the students' abilities at the end of the semester. The librarian and faculty member made minor changes to the questions in the pre- and post-test, since "it was a take-home assignment, giving students the opportunity to store the answers on their home computers and then copy and paste the answers into the post-test." The instructors created a rubric to score the pre-/post-tests and the post-tests counted toward the students' final course grades. Students were told that the pre-test was diagnostic and that the "assignment would be administered a second time, for a grade, near the end of the semester," which helped motivate them to complete it carefully. This particular pre-/post-test implementation is most interesting in how the test was designed, since it asked the students to answer six questions that required them to apply their skills in order to complete specific tasks, such as locating experts that they might want to interview and find reliable demographic and statistical information to support an argument. Pre-/post-tests are often structured as multiple-choice surveys rather than performance assessments. However, in this case the instructors at California State University, Long Beach, combined an authentic performance assessment with a pre-/post-test in order to determine whether students' information gathering skills, and thus information literacy competencies, actually improved over the course of the semester. In addition, because of the close collaboration between the faculty member and the librarian, they were able to implement the pre-/post-test in a course that included only one class taught by the librarian. Since the pre-/post-test was a take-home assignment, it needed no class time to administer. Instead, the instructors used the pre-test to help them understand the students' baseline knowledge and then geared their teaching toward helping students learn what they needed to know to success-fully complete the course and work as journalists—with the results indicating "that students' information-gathering skills improved."

The type of pre-/post-test that includes a performative task–based assignment has also been successfully employed to assess library competencies that are unique to specific areas of study. For example, because "music students need to navigate a complex network of printed music and sound recordings" (Myers and Ishimura 2016), librarians at Edith Cowan University developed an online tutorial, the "Music Library Instruction Module," which was originally designed as an optional "eLearning course written specifically for music students." The module focuses on the skills needed to locate both music scores and sound recordings within the library's collection, since "using the library catalog is a different user experience for the music student because of the unique characteristics of music in a library collection." In this case, both to evaluate the efficacy of the module and to assess the student learning that had taken place, the librarians designed a pre-/post-test that "mapped the search task to a learning outcome with an authentic need scenario." Students answered ten pre-test questions prior to working through the online module and then answered ten slightly different questions after completing the module, with each search task the same "but with variation in what the participant was asked to search for." The pre-/post-test questions asked students to search for the kinds of materials that they will need to successfully complete their program and included tasks such as searching the catalog by composer, identifying a sound recording and music score and noting the "shelf reference number" of each item. As we have seen, assessment instruments that ask students to perform "real-world" tasks not only reinforce their learning but also allow librarians to measure actual performance as opposed to short-term memory. In this case, the librarians at Edith Cowan found that the task-based pre-/post-test was able to measure student learning and that "there was significant change in ten search areas after module interaction, demon-strating an overall improvement in library search skills of first year music students." In addition, the data gathered from this authentic assessment instrument helped the librarians promote the module to outside stakeholders, including student orienta-tion and music teaching staff "for inclusion in Blackboard teaching units through embedding and linking," since they could demonstrate its effectiveness in improv-ing key information competencies.

As we have seen, problem-based learning and task-based activities are both effec-tive formative assessments as well as modes of teaching. In addition, they are both well suited for use with adult learners and other nontraditional students, which makes this approach ideally suited for community college libraries. For example, librarians teaching a one-hour-long research workshop at Arapahoe Community College designed the workshop to include problem-based learning scenarios and internet search strategies to teach information literacy skills that are relevant to the interests of nontraditional adult learners. In this case, "students completed a paper-based pretest before the workshop and a paper-based posttest following the workshop to measure their confidence levels, abilities in evaluating information, and perceived relevance of the workshop material" (Roberts 2017). Because the librarians wanted the session to be highly relevant for adult learners, they selected the session content "to focus on freely available resources that students might use after graduating or in their work or personal lives." In addition, the formal instruction was kept to a minimum, which allowed the students to spend most of their time practicing the skills needed to solve problem-based learning scenarios that required them to complete such information tasks as evaluating website credibility, finding open access materials, and locating historic news articles. The problem-based scenarios were open-ended, and students "could choose to discuss their strategies with those sitting nearby or to work individually if they preferred." After each scenario was completed, there was a brief class discussion in order to increase "students' metacognitive awareness of their research abilities." The pre-/post-test included both fill-in-the-blank and short-answer questions so that students were required to apply their knowledge, and the post-test included questions that "asked students to reflect on their own learning." In this case, the librarians were able to employ both formative and summative authentic assessment within a traditional one-shot session. By incorporating short-answer questions and a reflection component in the pre-/post-test, the instructors encouraged students to engage in higher-order thinking, and the practical problem-based approach added the real-world component that is essential for knowledge transfer. Most interestingly, on both the pre-test and post-test, the students were asked to evaluate two websites,

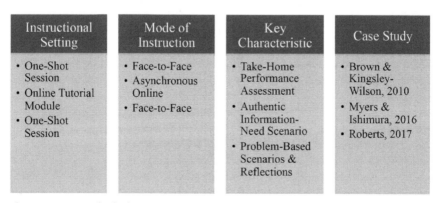

Instructional Setting	Mode of Instruction	Key Characteristic	Case Study
• One-Shot Session • Online Tutorial Module • One-Shot Session	• Face-to-Face • Asynchronous Online • Face-to-Face	• Take-Home Performance Assessment • Authentic Information-Need Scenario • Problem-Based Scenarios & Reflections	• Brown & Kingsley-Wilson, 2010 • Myers & Ishimura, 2016 • Roberts, 2017

Figure 4.11. Method of assessment: Pre-/post-tests. Jennifer S. Ferguson.

choose which was more reliable, and explain why. On the post-test, "students demonstrated a wider range of evaluation strategies" and "posttest comments indicated students used more than one criterion when considering a site," which was a marked improvement over the pre-test results. This outcome indicates both the efficacy of the session's mode of instruction and the real student learning that had taken place, since students needed to answer why questions rather than simply choose from a set of fixed answers. Moreover, the students in these sessions indicated that they found the skills they learned to be highly relevant, and as we have seen, this type of "innovative assessment" can help librarians to "demonstrate how information literacy skills contribute to greater metacognitive awareness and can be transferred to other concepts."

Presentations and Writing/Research Assignments

Because of their nature as summative assessments, longer-form writing/research assignments are most commonly employed in credit-bearing information literacy courses and embedded librarianship. In addition, because the implementation of writing/research assignments is closely related to best practices for annotated bibliographies, which have been previously described, a long discussion of their use in action will not be included here. Moreover, most discussions of information literacy using student papers as an assessment instrument focus on papers assigned in first-year writing or within discipline-specific courses, which makes it quite difficult to differentiate between faculty and librarian instruction, particularly if instruction is provided in a one-shot session. However, student presentations are a form of authentic summative assessment around which there has been little conversation but which merits some attention. For example, librarians at the University of Wyoming (UW) teach a three-credit information literacy course that addresses the university's general education plan, which includes an information literacy outcome. The UW librarians decided to offer an upper-level credit-bearing information literacy course in response to internal research demonstrating that most library instruction at the university took place at the first-year level and "students in upper-division classes are in greater need of in-depth library instruction, since they are more likely to be required to conduct research and write or present more than first-year students" (Mayer and Bowles-Terry 2013). Because they were teaching a semester-long credit-bearing course, the librarians were able to assess student learning in a number of ways, including a research project, a paper, and a presentation. In this case, the presentation was based on the research project and paper assignments, encouraging students to "reflect on what they learned over the course of the semester." In addition, students observed the presentations of their peers and were then required to write a brief "synthesis essay in which they must bring together at least two major themes of the class presentations and reflect on what they learned about the topic." The use of presentations in this course is particularly interesting in that this single assignment accomplished several tasks necessary to authentic assessment. First, the students had to analyze what they learned during the semester and then reflect on it, which prompted them to synthesize their knowledge and encouraged higher-order thinking. In addition, the students needed to apply their learning in order to both create their own presentations as well as to reflect on the presentations of their peers, thus encouraging peer learning, which was "helpful for students as they synthesize the new information they have gained in the class." While this particular type of assessment may be most suited to credit-bearing courses and embedded librarianship, aspects of it can be adapted to other settings. For example, in longer one-shot sessions, students can work together in teams to complete tasks or solve information problems, report out on their solutions, and provide peer feedback. While that type of presentation would be less formal than those assigned in semester-long courses, it would still include some of the key aspects of authentic assessment.

Student presentations have also been employed as an assessment technique within the context of problem-based learning in tiered information literacy programs. For example, a librarian at Chatham University collaborated with a faculty member to embed a problem-based information literacy assignment in a gender and contemporary issues course. The librarian and faculty member "worked together to create an outline of a PBL project to take place over five 75-minute class periods" toward the end of the semester (Wenger 2014). The class of twenty-four was divided into three groups of eight with the faculty member and librarian each facilitating one section and another librarian and master's student facilitating the third. In this case, "the facilitator promotes a student-centered approach by asking questions to encourage discussion and probe the students for information," and because the facilitator role does not require subject expertise, it is "easier for a librarian to serve as a facilitator in a course." Because the problem-based learning approach encourages students to evaluate themselves and each other throughout the process, authentic learning and assessment takes place continuously, with the facilitator questioning students about resources and search strategies rather than telling them what to use. Because "all students had attended a traditional lecture-based library instruction session the previous semester," the instructors hoped "that they would apply the information they had already learned in that session to the task at hand and then expand upon it." The final project for the information literacy sections of this course was a ten-minute group "presentation to raise awareness" of a particular issue and "convince their classmates of their issue's importance." Each group then received feedback from their fellow students, which they reviewed in order to determine how to revise them for the final class. In the final class, "each student group gave two presentations: one that was revised from the previous class and another that proposed a campaign to take action." This assignment is particularly interesting in that students were required to synthesize the information they located, and apply it to creating two different presentations; they were able to revise their work based on immediate and relevant feedback, since each group received prompts to guide their constructive and meaningful criticism of the others. Thus, the students had both a shared understanding of assessment criteria and an opportunity to apply the feedback to improving their learning.

Along with teaching credit-bearing information literacy classes and participating in embedded librarianship, librarians have also co-taught discipline-specific courses with faculty members in which presentations were used for assessment. This kind of co-teaching allows librarians to infuse these courses with information literacy concepts throughout the class with the subject-based content ensuring that most students will find the material more relevant than information literacy instruction alone. For example, at Ohio State University (OSU), the health sciences librarian "is the co-instructor in a required information literacy competencies course for first-year undergraduate students in the Honors Biomedical Science Major" (Powell and Ginier 2013). In this case, the librarian and a faculty member in anatomy teamed up to provide both subject expertise and to teach information literacy skills over two quarters of instruction with the goal that students are able to "master the biomedical literature" by the end of the period. The students in this course were divided into teams of three or four and were assigned one of six "signature programs," such as cancer, critical care, and neuroscience, on which the "OSU medical center's administrators and researchers have chosen to concentrate the institution's resources." The student teams then developed specific research topics within these broad biomedical categories to work on during the two quarters, with the librarian instructor teaching research skills and the faculty instructor teaching subject-based competencies. At the end of the first quarter, in which the librarian was the lead instructor, the "final projects were presentations by the student teams to their BMS instructors and classmates, in which they discussed 'the current state of the research' for their specific biomedical topics." The faculty member was the lead instructor for the second quarter, in which the students "did new literature searches on a research hypothesis in their specific topics," tested their hypothesis, and projected findings that might result. At the end of this quarter, "as their final projects, the student teams were required to present their research hypotheses, methodologies, and projected experimental results before their classmates and instructors and to produce supporting reference lists." In this

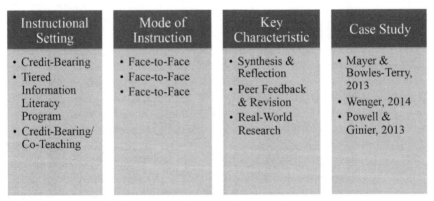

Instructional Setting	Mode of Instruction	Key Characteristic	Case Study
• Credit-Bearing • Tiered Information Literacy Program • Credit-Bearing/ Co-Teaching	• Face-to-Face • Face-to-Face • Face-to-Face	• Synthesis & Reflection • Peer Feedback & Revision • Real-World Research	• Mayer & Bowles-Terry, 2013 • Wenger, 2014 • Powell & Ginier, 2013

Figure 4.12.   Method of assessment: Presentations. Jennifer S. Ferguson.

case, students built on their previous research, were encouraged to revise their work, and were introduced to the ways in which scholarship develops over time, which not only modeled real-world research in their chosen field but also embedded authentic learning and information literacy assessment into the fabric of a required discipline-specific course.

Tests and Proficiency Projects

Proficiency projects resemble performative task-based assignments and problem-based learning activities in that they require students to apply their skills to complete a specific task or solve a real-world problem. As its name implies, proficiency projects are longer-form versions of task-based assignments and often require the application of a larger skill set than usually required for a shorter assignment. However, because of their similarity to both task-based assignments and problem-based activities, both of which have been previously described, a long discussion of their use in action will not be included in this section. In addition, authentic testing has been discussed in the section in this chapter that covers pre-/post-tests, and best practices for implementing authentic tests are outlined there; a longer discussion of their implementation can be found in that section. Thus, the sections in this chapter on performative task-based assignments, problem-based activities, and pre-/post-tests provide a number of examples that can be adapted to proficiency projects and authentic tests across instructional settings.

Search Logs

Search logs, also called research logs, in which students explain their search strategies and reflect on their information-seeking behaviors, are a form of summative assessment that can be implemented across a large number of instructional settings, from face-to-face one-shot sessions to credit-bearing asynchronous online instruction. For example, librarians at Anne Arundel Community College implemented a research log assignment within a credit-bearing online information literacy course. In this case, "students are required to complete research logs whenever they search for information on their topics, whether in catalogs, library databases, or on the web" (Whitlock and Nanavati 2013). This assignment asks the students to detail the process they used, the results they found, the reasons for the choices they made, questions they asked themselves along the way, and what happened when they performed the searches. In this way, students had to apply their knowledge of searching to complete a specific task, analyze the outcome of that task, and reflect on the reasoning behind their choices, which makes the research log a truly authentic assessment. In addition, "to prepare students for this learning activity and authentic assessment," instructors ideally should provide detailed directions for how to complete the assignment along with a grading rubric and example of a successfully completed research log, which helps students understand performance expectations and make sense of the feedback they receive from graded assignments. While the librarians note that "this is a long and arduous activity/assessment for students to complete and for instructors to score," it models a process that students need to learn and thus "it's best to assess process, rather than—or in addition to—the products that come out of it."

Search logs have also been used to assess information literacy competencies within the context of course-integrated online tutorial modules. For example, librarians at the University of Western Ontario transformed in-person library instruction for first-year engineering students to an online library module, which "was intended to be embedded as part of the ES1050 course site" within the course management system (Zhang, Goodman, and Shiyi 2015). Along with the online modules, the librarians also held several optional face-to-face tutorial sessions "to provide students with in-person research support." The library tutorial module was designed to help students with their course assignments, including a research report on a specific engineering topic, and included a "search log assignment to record their information searching process on their chosen topic." In this case, the tutorials introduced students to both general library information and engineering-specific research resources to help them complete their course assignments. This also helped enhance the tutorials' relevancy for students who could make a direct connection between the library content and their course content. Along with the course assignment, the students had to complete a search log to assess information literacy learning outcomes that "were designed to align with the five standards of the Information Literacy Standards for Science and Engineering/Technology." In addition to the online modules, students could choose to attend optional tutorial session(s), including sessions focused on individual tutorial modules such as "Designing Search Strategy" in order to "help students with their course-related research questions individually or in groups." The Western Ontario librarians found that focusing some of the tutorials on engineering-specific sources was helpful not only for the students completing their research reports but also for completing their search log assignments. In this case, the search logs acted as precursors to a final research report for which students received a grade; as we have seen, linking information literacy directly to discipline-specific learning helps students make connections and encourages knowledge transfer.

Librarians have also used research logs as an effective assessment instrument in situations where traditional first-year instruction has been replaced by or supplemented with online tutorials. For example, a librarian at California State University, Stanislaus, collaborated with an English department faculty member who "asked the librarian who normally conducts the in-person research skills session to develop something equivalent for his new online freshman composition course" (Held 2010). In the past, the librarian had provided a typical one-shot instruction session but recognized the need to change that model given the opportunity to embed tutorials into the course's learning management page. The librarian embedded a sequence of tutorials focused on the specific information literacy skills and abilities taught in the traditional face-to-face class and requested by the faculty member. In this case, the faculty member agreed to embed the content in a folder within the course assignment section that included links to the tutorials and contextual information that provided "a brief introduction to basic library services" followed with "ample library contacts in order to welcome student's questions." Each tutorial included embedded free-text questions that served as prompts for an iterative research log assignment. During the module's design phase, the faculty member "liked the idea of this research log, a set of reflections on the steps in the research process" because "it showed higher level learning in the analysis and synthesis that are necessary to make decisions about students' evolving topics based on what they learned in the tutorials." While the research log assignment was not mandatory, students who completed it were given a "check off" credit when they turned it in with their research papers. Interestingly, though not surprisingly, while the faculty member was satisfied with student responses to the research log questions, because the library assignment was not mandatory, some students failed to complete it. Thus, "he speculated that offering more than the 'check off' credit might engender more motivation." In this case, the faculty member and librarian agreed on the research log assignment because it could better demonstrate "higher level learning" than multiple-choice quizzes or other more standard methods of assessment used in online tutorials. In addition, the faculty member also confirmed that connecting information literacy learning outcomes more closely to discipline-specific goals increases its relevancy and the likelihood that students will complete assignments.

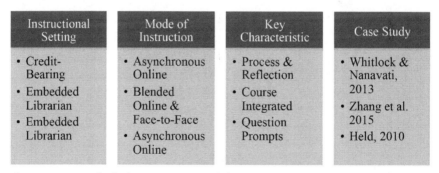

Instructional Setting	Mode of Instruction	Key Characteristic	Case Study
• Credit-Bearing • Embedded Librarian • Embedded Librarian	• Asynchronous Online • Blended Online & Face-to-Face • Asynchronous Online	• Process & Reflection • Course Integrated • Question Prompts	• Whitlock & Nanavati, 2013 • Zhang et al. 2015 • Held, 2010

Figure 4.13. Method of assessment: Search logs. Jennifer S. Ferguson.

Finally, the wide number of both formative and summative instruments available to librarians makes authentic assessment obtainable in every instructional setting, including one-shot sessions. This chapter can help librarians choose the assessment instrument that works best for their library and institutional needs. The next chapter will discuss the pedagogy of authentic assessment in order to help librarians understand how to integrate teaching, learning, and assessment across information literacy instructional contexts.

REFERENCES

Adams, Claudia, Stephen Buetow, Richard Edlin, Neda Zdravkovic, and Josta Heyligers. 2016. "A Collaborative Approach to Integrating Information and Academic Literacy into the Curricula of Research Methods Courses." *Journal of Academic Librarianship* 42, no. 3 (May) 222–31.

Brown, Carol Perruso, and Barbara Kingsley-Wilson. 2010. "Assessing Organically: Turning an Assignment into an Assessment." *Reference Services Review* 38, no. 4 (Winter): 536–56.

Burgoyne, Mary Beth, and Kim Chuppa-Cornell. 2015. "Beyond Embedded: Creating an Online-Learning Community Integrating Information Literacy and Composition Courses." *Journal of Academic Librarianship* 41, no. 4 (July): 416–21.

Carroll, Alexander J., Nedelina Tchangalova, and Eileen G. Harrington. 2016. "Flipping One-Shot Library Instruction: Using Canvas and Pecha Kucha for Peer Teaching." *Journal of the Medical Library Association* 104, no. 2 (April): 125–30.

Catalano, Amy. 2015. "The Effect of a Situated Learning Environment in a Distance Education Information Literacy Course." *Journal of Academic Librarianship* 41, no. 5 (September): 653–59.

Choinski, Elizabeth, and Michelle Emanuel. 2006. "The One-Minute Paper and the One-Hour Class: Outcomes Assessment for One-Shot Library Instruction." *Reference Services Review* 34, no. 1 (Spring): 148–55.

Cook, Peg, and Mary Walsh. 2012. "Collaboration and Problem-Based Learning." *Communications in Information Literacy* 6, no. 1 (March): 59–72.

Courtney, Michael, and Sara Wilhoite-Mathews. 2015. "From Distance Education to Online Learning: Practical Approaches to Information Literacy Instruction and Collaborative Learning in Online Environments." *Journal of Library Administration* 55, no. 4 (May): 261–77.

Gariepy, Laura W., Jennifer A. Stout, and Megan L. Hodge. 2016. "Using Rubrics to Assess Learning in Course-Integrated Library Instruction." *Portal: Libraries and the Academy* 16, no. 3 (July): 491–509.

Gustavson, Amy. 2012. "Using ILIAC to Systematically Plan and Implement a Library Information Literacy Assessment Program for Freshman Classes." *Public Services Quarterly* 8, no. 2 (April–June): 97–113.

Halpern, Rebecca, and Chimene Tucker. 2015. "Leveraging Adult Learning Theory with Online Tutorials." *Reference Services Review* 43, no. 1 (Spring): 112–24.

Hawes, Sandra Lee, and Jane Mason Adamson. 2016. "Flipping Out over Online Library Instruction: A Case Study in Faculty-Librarian Collaboration." *Journal of Library and Information Services in Distance Learning* 10, nos. 3–4 (July–December): 254–67.

Held, Tim. 2010. "Blending In: Collaborating with an Instructor in an Online Course." *Journal of Library & Information Services in Distance Learning* 4, no. 4 (October–December): 153–65.

Hoffmann, Debra, and Kristen LaBonte. 2012. "Meeting Information Literacy Outcomes: Partnering with Faculty to Create Effective Information Literacy Assessment." *Journal of Information Literacy* 6, no. 2 (December): 70–85.

Jarrell, Lisa. 2014. "Meeting in the Middle: Assessment Ideals and Campus Realities." *Indiana Libraries* 33 (2): 37–40.

Kim, Miseon, and Michael Dolan. 2015. "'Excuse Me, but What Is a Research Paper?': Embedded Librarian Program and Information Literacy Skills of Community College Students." *Community & Junior College Libraries* 21, no. 1/2, (January/June): 53–70.

Loo, Jeffery L., David Eifler, Elliott Smith, Liladhar Pendse, Jianye He, Michael Sholinbeck, Gisele Tanasse, Jennifer K. Nelson, and Elizabeth A. Dupuis. 2016. "Flipped Instruction for Information Literacy: Five Instructional Cases of Academic Librarians." *Journal of Academic Librarianship* 42, no. 3 (May): 273–80.

Martin, Jennifer R., and Marion K. Slack. 2013. "Using Focus Groups to Assess the Information Literacy Skills of First-Year Pharmacy Students." Presentation at the Annual Conference of the Special Libraries Association, San Diego, June 9–11.

Martin, Lisa. 2015. "Assessing Student Learning during Information Literacy Sessions for Large Business Classes." *Journal of Business and Finance Librarianship* 20, no. 4 (October–December): 330–38.

Mayer, Jennifer, and Melissa Bowles-Terry. 2013. "Engagement and Assessment in a Credit-Bearing Information Literacy Course." *Reference Services Review* 41, no. 1 (Spring): 62–79.

McGonigal, Kelly. 2005. "Using Class Discussion to Meet Your Teaching Goals." *Speaking of Teaching* 15, no. 1 (Fall): 1–6.

Myers, Amanda, and Yusuke Ishimura. 2016. "Finding Sound and Score: A Music Library Skills Module for Undergraduate Students." *Journal of Academic Librarianship* 42, no. 3 (May): 215–21.

Natalle, Elizabeth J., and Kathryn M. Crowe. 2013. "Information Literacy and Communication Research: A Case Study on Interdisciplinary Assessment." *Communication Education* 62, no. 1 (January): 97–104.

Oliver, John Thomas. 2015. "One-Shot Wikipedia: An Edit-Sprint toward Information Literacy." *Reference Services Review* 43, no. 1 (Spring): 81–97.

Pashia, Angela, and Jessica Critten. 2015. "Ethnography as Pedagogy in Library Orientations." *Journal of Information Literacy* 9, no. 2 (December): 84–93.

Powell, Carol A., and Emily C. Ginier. 2013. "Lessons Learned: Year-by-Year Improvement of a Required Information Competency Course." *Medical Reference Services Quarterly* 32, no. 3 (July–September): 290–313.

Rapchak, Marcia, and Robert Behary. 2013. "Digital Immigrants, Digital Learning: Reaching Adults through Information Literacy Instruction Online." *Journal of Library and Information Services in Distance Learning* 7, no. 4 (October–December): 349–59.

Rapchak, Marcia E., Leslie A. Lewis, Julie K. Motyka, and Margaret Balmert. 2015. "Information Literacy and Adult Learners." *Adult Learning* 26, no. 4 (November): 135–42.

Roberts, Lindsay. 2017. "Research in the Real World: Improving Adult Learners Web Search and Evaluation Skills through Motivational Design and Problem-Based Learning." *College and Research Libraries* 78, no. 4 (May): 527–51.

Seeber, Kevin P. 2013. "Using Assessment Results to Reinforce Campus Partnerships." *College and Undergraduate Libraries* 20, no. 3/4 (July/December): 352–65.

Sen, Barbara A., and Pamela McKinney. 2014. "The SEA-change Model in Information Literacy: Assessing Information Literacy Development with Reflective Writing." *Nordic Journal of Information Literacy in Higher Education* 6 (1): 6–22.

Sharma, Shikha. 2007. "From Chaos to Clarity: Using the Research Portfolio to Teach and Assess Information Literacy Skills." *Journal of Academic Librarianship* 33, no. 1 (January): 127–35.

Sharman, Alison. 2017. "Using Ethnographic Research Techniques to Find Out the Story behind International Student Library Usage in the Library Impact Data Project." *Library Management* 38 (1): 2–10.

Smith, Meggan D., and Amy B. Dailey. 2013. "Improving and Assessing Information Literacy Skills through Faculty-Librarian Collaboration." *College and Undergraduate Libraries* 20, no. 3/4 (July): 314–26.

Snavely, Loanne L., and Carol A. Wright. 2003. "Research Portfolio Use in Undergraduate Honors Education: Assessment Tool and Model for Future Work." *Journal of Academic Librarianship* 29, no. 5 (September): 298–303.

Sonley, Valerie, Denise Turner, Sue Myer, and Yvonne Cotton. 2007. "Information Literacy Assessment by Portfolio: A Case Study." *Reference Services Review* 35, no. 1 (Spring): 41–70.

Squibb, Sara Davidson, and Susan Mikkelsen. 2016. "Assessing the Value of Course-Embedded Information Literacy on Student Learning and Achievement." *College and Research Libraries* 77, no. 2 (March): 164–83.

Wenger, Kate. 2014. "Problem-Based Learning and Information Literacy." *Pennsylvania Libraries: Research and Practice* 2, no. 2 (Fall): 142–54.

Wheeler, Diana, Lia Vellardita, and Amy Kindschi. 2010. "Providing a Credit Information Literacy Course for an Engineering School." In *Best Practices for Credit-Bearing Information Literacy Courses*, edited by Christopher V. Hollister, 109–25. Chicago: Association of College and Research Libraries.

Whitlock, Brandy, and Julie Nanavati. 2013. "A Systematic Approach to Performative and Authentic Assessment." *Reference Services Review* 41, no. 1 (Spring): 32–48.

Wolstenholme, Jackie. 2015. "Evidence Based Practice Using Formative Assessment in Library Research Support." *Evidence Based Library and Information Practice* 10, no. 3 (September): 4–29.

Zhang, Qinqin, Maren Goodman, and Xie Shiyi. 2015. "Integrating Library Instruction into the Course Management System for a First-Year Engineering Class: An Evidence-Based Study Measuring the Effectiveness of Blended Learning on Students' Information Literacy Levels." *College and Research Libraries* 76, no. 7 (November): 934–58.

5

Authentic Assessment in Context

Authentic assessment requires instruction librarians to align their teaching with the assessment instruments since authentic assessment is as much about learning as it is about assessment. Employing common assessment instruments such as traditional multiple-choice quizzes requires only that instruction librarians convey information to students who then demonstrate, at least in the short term, whether they remembered the content conveyed. However, "teaching to the authentic test" can present a challenge, especially if an instructor is new to this field, as it often requires librarians to become proficient with important aspects of instructional design in order to activate students' higher-order thinking and the kind of learning that promotes knowledge transfer. This chapter will discuss some of the key components of effective teaching and instructional design and highlight case studies that illustrate best practices for the pedagogy of authentic assessment within the most common instructional contexts.

CREDIT-BEARING COURSES

As we have seen, librarians teaching credit-bearing courses—both subject-based and library-specific—have a number of both formative and summative assessments available to them. In both cases, good instructional design can encourage significant student learning and promote knowledge transfer. This knowledge transfer is especially important when credit-bearing classes include only library-specific content, since a student's ability to retain that content and transfer the information-seeking and evaluative techniques they learn to their discipline-specific courses is the entire point of credit-bearing information literacy instruction. When credit-bearing information literacy instruction is fully integrated within a particular discipline, students can more easily understand the relevance of the course material to their major area of study, which helps students assimilate information literacy skills more easily into their subject-based coursework. With this added layer of difficulty in mind, this section focuses on credit-bearing information literacy courses that do not include discipline-specific content and discusses both online and face-to-face instruction. For example, the librarians at Hofstra University who successfully employed discussion boards as an authentic assessment used a "situated learning" model to design the credit-bearing distance education information literacy course in which they were implemented. The Hofstra librarians based their instructional design on situated cognition, which is "a theory that proposes that learning is inseparable from authentic activity" and employs a teaching strategy known as cognitive apprenticeship "in which an 'expert' (the teacher) models a skill" (Catalano 2015). While this approach has rarely been discussed in the library literature, it has been widely discussed in other disciplines, with the concept of situated learning and cognitive apprenticeship thought to "have the potential to produce transferable knowledge." Interestingly, the main principles of cognitive apprenticeship include "expert modeling, authentic activities, and facilitating the generalization of these activities so that they may be used in other situations," thus promoting knowledge transfer. In this case, the Hofstra librarians designed a credit-bearing online information literacy course that used cognitive apprenticeship to incorporate problem-based learning into distance education in order to focus on teaching for transfer. The "instruction incorporated the elements of situated learning and teaching for transfer," in which, instead of lecturing, the instructor modeled tasks, including evaluation, explaining "how she would consider each criterion for evaluation for each source—thus modeling how an expert might select sources appropriate for research projects." At Hofstra, this type of modeling helped students understand information literacy concepts in a more concrete way, since observing the librarian apply knowledge to completing a task provided students with a model for how to apply their own newly acquired knowledge to solve important research-based problems across disciplines. This type of instructional design encourages knowledge transfer, one of the most important components of higher-order thinking and learning. In addition, this type of instruction also avoids the kind of simplistic dualities—good versus bad—which are often employed in library instruction, since "if students are taught only to use a checklist to determine credibility, they may never learn to apply the concept of evaluation to sources encountered in the real world." As we have seen, focusing on teaching concepts rather than mechanics encourages students to develop a greater awareness of how their knowledge and skills apply, as the Hofstra librarians observe, across "different contexts or with different materials," which is the essence of knowledge transfer. Because of this teaching strategy, the Hofstra librarians found that recontextualizing information literacy concepts optimized the potential for transfer and that "allowing students to practice the knowledge in different situations or contexts better prepares them to apply the knowledge to a real-life situation." Given its potential to promote lifelong learning, this particular methodology both promotes authentic learning and also provides librarians with powerful assessment data that reinforces many of the outcomes most important to key stakeholders in higher education.

Powerful instructional design concepts can also be implemented in face-to-face instruction within credit-bearing courses. For example, the librarians at Duquesne University who instruct nontraditional adult students designed their credit-bearing courses to work within both the online and face-to-face instructional contexts. In this case, they incorporated adult learning theory and designed the course with the characteristics of adult learners in mind in order to leverage this theory to create a more significant learning experience for their students. After their initial implementation, the librarians found that nontraditional adult students responded best to "a new technique of modeling appropriate evaluations of sources and providing timely feedback to students" (Rapchak et al. 2015). In addition, the students benefited from the instructor scaffolding each task and providing templates of successful assignments that helped students understand the components of critical evaluation. The Duquesne case confirms that nontraditional students, whether adult learners or international students, often benefit significantly from instructors both modeling evaluative techniques and providing examples of successfully completed assignments, since these students enter higher education with a wide array of experiences with both finding and critically appraising information sources in order to construct an argument or solve a problem. After revising instruction to include these elements, among other high-impact practices, the librarians at Duquesne found that "many students scored higher in the evaluation section and their overall capstone projects," and they go on to "recommend [that] instructors, regardless of discipline, model and scaffold appropriate IL learning outcomes, especially evaluating information." In addition to scaffolding instruction and modeling techniques, the librarians at

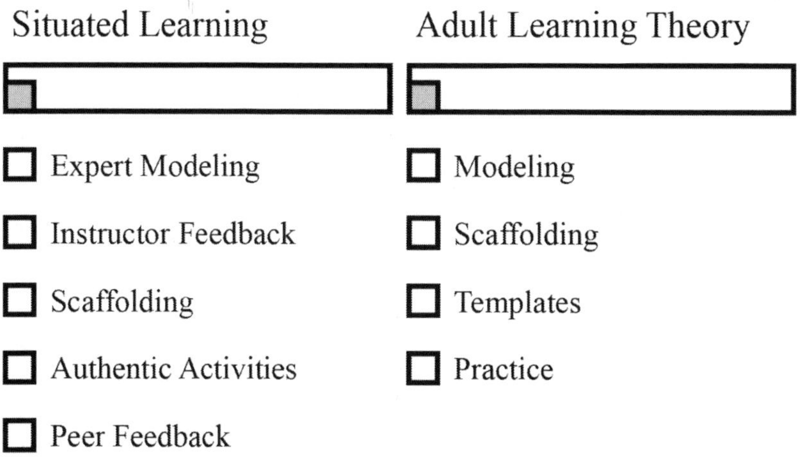

Situated Learning   Adult Learning Theory

☐ Expert Modeling   ☐ Modeling

☐ Instructor Feedback   ☐ Scaffolding

☐ Scaffolding   ☐ Templates

☐ Authentic Activities   ☐ Practice

☐ Peer Feedback

Figure 5.1.   Instructional setting: Credit-bearing courses. Jennifer S. Ferguson.

Duquesne also confirmed that adult learners find "that direct practice in courses is most beneficial to their learning," which reinforces the idea that providing meaningful feedback and allowing students to revise their work based on that feedback is essential in order to convey the iterative nature of the research process and promote higher-order thinking. Interestingly, the librarians at Hofstra working with traditional undergraduates and the librarians at Duquesne working with nontraditional adult learners both found that directly connecting information literacy to practical needs, whether through problem-based learning or emphasizing its relevance to students' coursework, was the "surest way to motivate knowledge acquisition."

EMBEDDED LIBRARIANSHIP

Because embedded librarians have more access to students, whether through providing multiple instruction sessions or having a presence within an online course page, their ability to implement authentic assessment instruments resembles that of credit-bearing courses. However, even with multiple instruction sessions, embedded librarians still need to adjust their teaching methods and instructional design to compensate for providing fewer sessions than students would receive in a credit-bearing course. Given that limitation, embedded librarians have used a number of instructional strategies to convey a significant amount of information within a limited time frame. For example, the librarians at Queensborough Community College (QCC) who implemented annotated bibliographies within an embedded librarian program used scaffolding to align each of three information literacy classes with student learning outcomes. In this case, the "embedded library information literacy classes were designed to provide students with step by step instructions so they were able to incorporate what they learned into their research papers at their own pace and with plenty of preparation for their final draft" (Kim and Dolan 2015). As noted earlier, adult and other nontraditional students often benefit from breaking information into easily digestible chunks that they can approach at their own pace. At QCC, each of the three sessions concentrated on one learning outcome, from understanding the difference between an essay and a research paper to understanding information ethics and the value of proper citations. Equally importantly, the students were provided with a significant amount of time for hands-on practice during each session to hone their skills while a librarian was present to answer questions and encourage revision. As a result of implementing scaffolded instruction within an embedded program, the QCC librarians discovered that it was just as essential to define "what a research paper is" as it was to provide instruction on keyword searching, thus confirming that scaffolded instruction needs to start with the basics in order to build on a strong, mutually understood foundation. Equally interestingly, this program also confirmed that instruction that focuses more broadly on a limited number of information seeking concepts rather than mechanics and includes "more hands-on class activities" is more effective and promotes student learning in a more authentic way. In addition, their experience also confirmed that "students were most likely to have lower IL skills than they had believed," which confirms the importance of authentic assessment of information literacy, since student self-assessments and individually reported confidence levels often do not reflect their actual skills. Not surprisingly, "overall, students did not take library instruction seriously because they confused digital literacy with information literacy," and they believed that because they could find information on the internet they could also find reliable scholarly information in the same way. Scaffolding instruction can help students understand the difference between finding information and conducting college-level research and writing. If nothing else, this method can help students begin to understand what they do not know, which can have a significant impact on learning.

Understanding students' prior knowledge and addressing gaps in understanding are key aspects of authentic teaching and assessment, and librarians at the University of Notre Dame Australia used a Wikipedia editing exercise to help them understand whether students could confirm their reported self-confidence in actual practice. In this case, librarians partner with the unit coordinator on a required course for first-year health sciences students, Academic Research and Writing in the Health Sciences, to embed information literacy within the course. In order to provide both a meaningful learning experience for students and an authentic assessment, the Notre Dame librarians employed "an action research process commonly used in higher education as a systematic intervention to improve pedagogical practice" (Dawe and Robinson 2017). Action research helps instructors identify a problem, design an intervention to solve the problem, implement the intervention, and evaluate the results—which "promotes an evidence-based way of approaching teaching practice." In this case, action research helped the Notre Dame librarians redesign their delivery of information literacy instruction for first-year health science students, since the standard lecture-tutorial structure they had previously employed did not seem to help students complete the annotated bibliography assignment, where they failed "to understand its connection to the subsequent essay and would produce poor-quality annotated bibliographies that failed to serve the desired purpose." Instead, the librarians redesigned both the pedagogical approach and the assessment, moving to a Wikipedia editing exercise that used problem-based learning in order to engage students in a more authentic way. In this case, after evaluating their methods using the action research process, the instructors "agreed that students still needed an assignment that would help prepare them for the essay by introducing them to scholarly information sources and giving them a chance to practise referencing and paraphrasing"; they designed an assessment "around Wikipedia editing, with a focus on Australian health issues." Instead of having the students create an annotated bibliography, the librarians taught their students to "identify a gap in the Wikipedia literature, propose their topic and write and publish an article." This exercise helped the students connect each step of instruction to their final essay and also understand how the scholarly conversation is developed. Because creating a Wikipedia entry is "an authentic learning task," students experienced "peer review and publishing in an

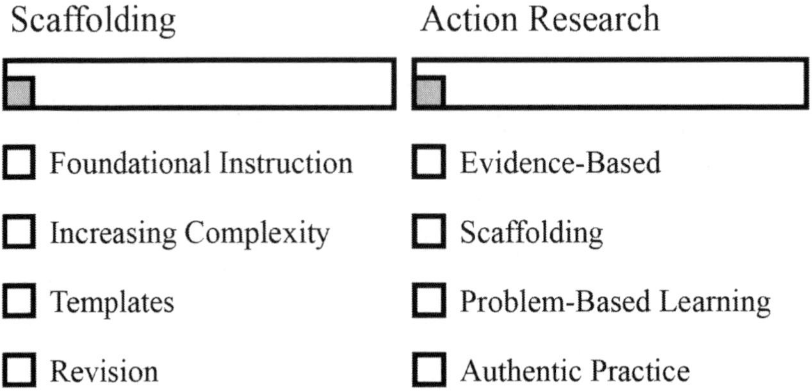

Scaffolding   Action Research

☐ Foundational Instruction   ☐ Evidence-Based

☐ Increasing Complexity   ☐ Scaffolding

☐ Templates   ☐ Problem-Based Learning

☐ Revision   ☐ Authentic Practice

Figure 5.2. Instructional setting: Embedded librarianship. Jennifer S. Ferguson.

essential resource" at first hand, which engaged them "by highlighting the importance of creating, rather than merely consuming, information." This emphasis on the creation of information is especially important given the need for students to demonstrate not only information literacy but also metaliteracy, which accentuates the heterogeneity of information literacy and encourages proficiencies not only in finding and synthesizing information but also in creating information (Mackey and Jacobson 2011).

COLLABORATIONS

Faculty-librarian collaboration can often result in significant opportunities to improve teaching and learning, since both partners benefit from leveraging each other's domain of expertise. In this case, librarians may learn about new and more effective approaches to teaching, while faculty members may begin to better understand the complexities of information literacy as well as the limitations of most students' information-seeking behaviors. Indeed, discipline-specific faculty members are often surprised by what students do not know about how to find and evaluate information sources; they assume that because students are relatively technically proficient that they are also information literate. However, nothing could be farther from the experience of teaching librarians. Thus, faculty-librarian collaboration can strongly benefit all involved and result in enhanced student learning. For example, a librarian at Saint Leo University collaborated with a member of the graduate faculty "to develop a flipped classroom library instruction session for students who were taking an online graduate course in instructional design" (Hawes and Adamson 2016). These collaborators employed Universal Design for Learning (UDL), which "essentially provides multiple means of representation, engagement, and expression" to develop learning objects, which students completed outside of class. These learning objects included short video tutorials, slideshows, audio clips, and text-based instruction. In addition to providing students with multiple formats, the tutorials in each module were quite short "in an attempt to place each tutorial within the context of the larger learning objective for the module." This type of flipped classroom model encouraged a "form of self-directed learning, incorporating the need for students to reflect upon the activities and draw conclusions about better ways to conduct their research in the future as a result of their experimentation in the worksheets (guided practice)." These modules were introduced to students early in the course, and the hands-on activities included in them were "grounded in a real-life context" to increase their relevancy to student coursework and promote knowledge transfer. The material was scaffolded so that each module was "directly related to the task at hand." In addition, each tutorial modeled a specific procedure and required students to practice what had been modeled by engaging with a set of exercises that reinforced the instructional materials. After completing the information literacy modules outside of class, the students then attended a live webinar in which the librarian could reinforce student learning by providing additional "hands-on exploration of the resources and skills" and answer any remaining questions. This example includes many of the key components of authentic teaching and learning, including prioritizing hands-on practice over instruction, breaking the modules into smaller problem-based chunks, and providing feedback to reinforce learning. In addition, because the librarian and faculty member collaborated closely on content and provided real-life context for the information literacy components, they found that this instructional model "successfully taught graduate students the necessary research and information literacy skills" that they need to succeed, "not only in the instructor's class, but also within the degree program."

In addition to faculty-librarian collaboration in an online course using the flipped classroom model, a librarian at Sam Houston State University collaborated with a faculty member on a "micro-presence" in an online graduate course in history, "working closely with the professor to review the learning outcome objectives of every course unit, discuss the information literacy aspects of those objectives, and outline accompanying library instructional materials to support students at every step" (Cassidy and Hendrickson 2013). Because the librarian participated in developing course-learning objectives, "course assignments were designed to scaffold the research and writing tasks that students were expected to master." In addition, the librarian was able to integrate into the course a "series of information literacy lessons and exercises for students to consume at will," which allowed them to pursue self-directed learning at their point of need. Moreover, the librarian's presence throughout the course encouraged students to "examine critically the success (or lack thereof) of their information-seeking activities," which can be especially important as the "scope and rigor" of each assignment increased, requiring students to demonstrate "more sophisticated skills of information discovery and evaluation." Most interestingly, in this case the librarian and faculty member shared a "virtual office" in the learning management system, which increased the librarian's visibility to students as well as laying the "groundwork for the expectation that the librarian would serve as a collaborative educator in the course." This point is especially crucial since student perceptions of authority can often be "administrative" in nature, recognizing that faculty members have the power to assign a grade (Meszaros 2010). When the librarian occupies the same space as that administrative authority, it can help endow the librarian with whatever authority the faculty member has, which at the very least, may convey to students that the content they are teaching has some value. In this case, the librarian understood that this perception of authority was important for student learning and so "took advantage of several key opportunities during the semester to send emails to the class, just as the professor was doing, to proactively inform or remind them" of important information or to ask "thought-provoking questions about their research process." In addition, the librarian at Sam Houston State also split the instruction into smaller, tailored modules that directly related to the information literacy needs of each specific assignment in order to better correspond to the students' points of need and included "interactive practice exercises" as well as multiple instructional formats, including short videos and informational graphics. Taken together, this method provided online students with a noteworthy learning experience, incorporating many elements of UDL along with performative tasks, self-directed learning, ongoing feedback, and opportunities to practice and revise, with all of the learning activities directly related to authentic course assignments. Thus, this particular case provides a good example of "teaching to the authentic test," in which information literacy instruction is inextricably integrated with discipline-specific coursework, and each assignment builds on and reinforces both subject knowledge and information literacy competencies.

Flipped Classroom   Micro-Presence

Flipped Classroom	Micro-Presence
☐ Universal Design for Learning	☐ Scaffolding
☐ Self-Efficacy	☐ Discipline Integrated
☐ Guided Practice	☐ Self-Directed Learning
☐ Scaffolding	☐ Multiple Instructional Formats

Figure 5.3.   Instructional setting: Collaborations. Jennifer S. Ferguson.

INFORMATION LITERACY PROGRAMS

Information literacy programs, whether semester-long or tiered throughout a student's academic career, offer librarians multiple points of contact with students during their course of study. Tiered information literacy programs are by their nature scaffolded, presenting increasingly sophisticated information as students progress through the program. For example, librarians at Middlesex University who work with computing students in the School of Science and Technology first provide an introductory two-hour workshop that teaches students the basics of keyword searching and evaluation and includes a section on resource evaluation. This workshop "is followed in the second and third year by further workshops which build on existing knowledge and skills" (Rahanu et al. 2016). At Middlesex, "Liaison Librarians are aligned to programmes and academic departments," and they are responsible for teaching information literacy at all levels in those programs and departments. Thus the instruction is fully integrated within the curriculum, which means that content can vary widely given the variety of information needs across disciplines. "For example Product Design students have three sessions in their first year, while in other programmes, the only formal contact with a Librarian is during Induction Week." However, the librarians working with each of these programs approach the teaching of information literacy in a similar way, and "the model developed by Middlesex LSS facilitates student involvement by using games and other activities, and by focussing workshops on a central project theme relevant to the student group." In this case, "games and activities are used throughout to encourage engagement, interaction and peer learning." These games and activities "include a card sorting exercise designed to encourage students to think about the range of resources available to them and how these can be used in their academic work." An additional activity "uses images to help students devise effective search terms in order to find information." Ideally, these workshops are "delivered by a synergistic collaboration between the academic staff," which includes faculty, and the librarians. In this case, the Middlesex librarians structure their workshops so that they include a number of authentic activities, such as peer learning, hands-on practice, curriculum-integrated instruction, and multiple modes of representation, and "the development of these games and activities led to the Librarians supporting computing being nominated for a Times Higher Education Leadership and Management Award in 2014." This case is a particularly interesting example of learner-centered teaching in a library context, emphasizing both "the active and reflective nature of learning and learners" (APA 1997). For example, the card sorting exercise actively engages students while also encouraging them to reflect on how they might use a particular resource in their academic work and share their insights with their peers. This deceptively simple lesson, which can be easily adapted to multiple instructional settings, engages both the instructor and the student in a collaborative learning experience, allowing both teacher and learner to think more deeply about the sources and uses of information.

In addition to information literacy programs designed to serve undergraduates, librarians have also developed tiered instruction models for specific disciplines and even specific programs. For example, librarians at California State University East Bay designed and implemented an information literacy program for the TESOL master of arts (MA) program at their university. In this case, the TESOL program's foundational goals include outcomes for "lifelong learning and developing information competency," which are "as central to information literacy as they are to the information competency goals for TESOL programs, teachers, and students" (Soules et al. 2013). Faculty-librarian collaboration on developing this program "began with a consideration of the students in the program" who were mainly nontraditional, including international students and adult learners; their "undergraduate preparations vary widely, their ages vary widely, and their native languages vary widely." As we have seen, this situation represents an increasingly common challenge for teaching librarians as the student population continues to change and assumptions about students' prior knowledge may not necessarily be valid. In response to these varying degrees of experience, the East Bay information literacy program evolved into learning communities, in which faculty, librarians, and the students themselves mentored each other and created an "enriching professional community." In addition to the more standard faculty-librarian collaboration in which both "act as mentors for each other's fields," the learning communities in this program included both the faculty member and teaching librarian mentoring the MA students "by engaging them in information literacy activities that mirror activities they will do as independent language teaching professionals." Along with these authentic, real-world activities, students are required to complete information literacy assignments that include reflective essays, providing students with multiple authentic teaching and learning objects that promote knowledge transfer. Moreover, the MA students also "have the opportunity to mentor each other" as well as to mentor the faculty member and librarian "through their search for and evaluation of language teaching and learning web sites." Most interestingly, in order to increase the relevancy and impact of the information literacy program, the faculty member and librarian analyzed students' reflective essays in order to determine where the program was succeeding or failing, where students understood concepts or continued to struggle. This process of revision used the authentic assessment instruments both to measure student learning and to improve teaching and instructional design. The learning community model enabled the librarian to reach students throughout their program of study and to gain a deeper understanding of their professional needs, thus leading to "a more programmatic approach to building information literacy skills through professionally relevant activities and assignments over a period of time." Because the assignments and activities were "professionally relevant," once students graduate from the program they are more likely to be "well prepared to embed information literacy in their language-learning curriculum, in ways that meet the language use and information needs of their own students." Indeed, confirming the instructors' conclusions, one student in the program reflected that "understanding how to filter, track, and evalu-

Learner-Centered Teaching   Learning Community

☐ Active Learning   ☐ Mentoring

☐ Reflection & Revision   ☐ Knowledge Sharing

☐ Problem-Based Activities   ☐ Real-Life Activities

☐ Synergistic   ☐ Peer-to-Peer Instruction

Figure 5.4.   Instructional setting: Information literacy programs. Jennifer S. Ferguson.

ate information is an important part of what an academic writer needs to be able to do," and went on to say that "this kind of understanding is something I am working to develop in my own students as they learn to write for academic audiences and use outside sources appropriately and effectively in that writing."

ONE-SHOT SESSIONS

Because one-shot sessions are by far the most common setting for information literacy instruction, the literature on pedagogy for one-shot sessions is quite extensive and ranges from the traditional bibliographic instruction session of the pre-internet age to the latest techniques for designing digital objects for asynchronous online instruction. Therefore, this section will not provide a history of one-shot library instruction sessions but will instead highlight authentic teaching and learning techniques that most librarians would be able to apply within this context. For example, the librarians at Arapahoe Community College who implemented problem-based learning used "Keller's ARCS Model of Motivational Design (Attention, Relevance, Confidence, and Satisfaction)" (Roberts 2017) to create a one-shot session that was relevant and resulted in authentic student learning. In this case, following this model, the librarians designed their instruction to include all four categories, starting with capturing students' attention at the beginning of the lesson through connecting the upcoming instruction to their prior knowledge. Using problem-based learning, the librarians then made the lesson relevant by concentrating instruction "on freely available resources that students might use after graduating or in their work or personal lives." To increase the students' confidence levels, the librarians provided short, scaffolded instruction followed by significant time for hands-on practice at each stage of the lesson. In addition, "students could choose to discuss their strategies

with those sitting nearby or to work individually if they preferred," since adult learners prefer to choose their own working styles. Moreover, as we have seen, "metalit-
erate learners" will increasingly be asked to "engage in social learning," which also
reinforces the need for more authentic teaching and learning in an environment that
requires many workers to engage with, synthesize, and create new information. Thus,
the Arapahoe librarians used motivational design and problem-based learning to "increase students' metacognitive awareness of their research abilities" and enable them
to transfer their knowledge beyond the classroom. Most interestingly, the techniques
used in this case "followed a conceptual approach that is closer to threshold concepts
than the ACRL Standards" thereby demonstrating that one-shot instruction sessions
can move beyond traditional point-and-click and promote higher-order thinking
and learning by teaching a limited number of broad concepts and allowing students
time to practice and reflect. Addressing each of the four categories of motivational
design during instruction enabled the instructors to focus on key information literacy concepts, empower their students to become better researchers, and help prepare
"a workforce that can successfully navigate the internet and make decisions from the
wealth of available information."

Along with adult and other nontraditional learners, librarians have also designed
one-shot sessions for traditional undergraduates that engage with authentic teaching
and learning. For example, librarians at McGill University designed student-centered
one-shot information literacy sessions by using student-generated content to inform
their instruction. In this case, they started each session by asking the students to
"write down a 'burning question' they had about the library or about library research.
The questions were then collected, quickly read by the librarian, and used to inform
the content of the workshop" (Hanz and Lange 2013). Students submitted their
questions anonymously, which helped limit potential embarrassment and provide
some reassurance when multiple students had the same question. These questions
provided the framework around which librarians built each workshop, which made
each session not only more "student-focused and student-driven" but also provided
instruction customized to the needs of each class. In addition, the librarians using
this technique were able to change their teaching methods in response to class needs
and to incorporate additional authentic elements into the session, such as providing
time "for students to locate answers to their colleague's questions before the librarian
does." Thus, in this case the session was not only student-driven but also provided
opportunities for hands-on practice, trial and error, and peer instruction. In addition,
this method was used in general rather than course-integrated instruction, making it
easily adaptable to introductory library sessions and library orientations for first-year
students. Most interestingly, after "each workshop, the students' questions were re-
corded for further analysis," which helped the librarians anticipate student needs and
correct some of their assumptions around what students know about library research.
In addition, this activity "also illuminated students' perspectives on the library and
highlighted some of the key areas in which library services could be improved." This
point is particularly interesting in that librarians using this method can track student

questions over time as a way to assess library service, as well as to promote authentic student learning. In addition, as higher education attempts to become increasingly student-centered, the nature of this method speaks to the concerns of institutional stakeholders, allowing librarians to close the loop between student needs, student learning, and library service, which can help communicate the library's impact on that learning, as well as the continual improvement of its services.

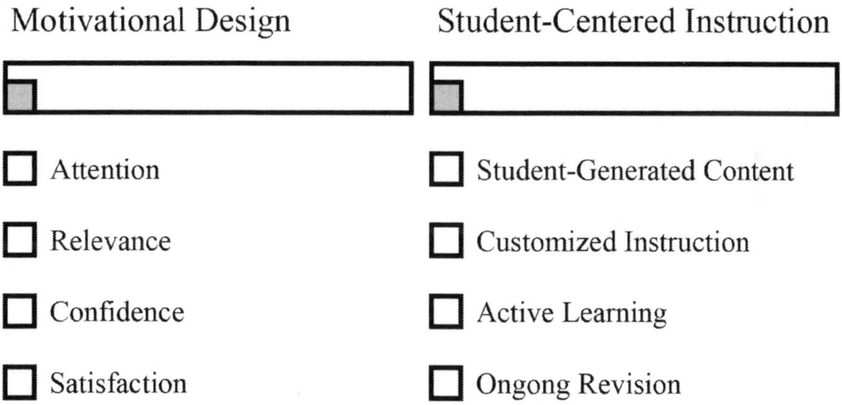

Motivational Design   Student-Centered Instruction

☐ Attention   ☐ Student-Generated Content

☐ Relevance   ☐ Customized Instruction

☐ Confidence   ☐ Active Learning

☐ Satisfaction   ☐ Ongong Revision

Figure 5.5.   Instructional setting: One-shot sessions. Jennifer S. Ferguson.

ONLINE INSTRUCTION

Because online instruction can take place across a large number of library instruction settings, including credit-bearing courses, embedded librarianship, and even one-shot sessions, this section will concentrate on cases where asynchronous online modules have been incorporated into more traditional information literacy settings and where they can be readily adapted to a number of contexts. For example, librarians at MacEwan University were concerned about the sustainability of their information literacy programming for a required first-year English course. The English subject librarian was unable to meet all of the demand for face-to-face instruction for this course, since it was a requirement for all students in every program at the university, but was reluctant to transition to an entirely online information literacy program, fearing that both the richness of face-to-face instruction and strong faculty relationships would be lost. With those concerns in mind, the librarians developed a blended model in which students completed mandatory online tutorials, determining that "basic search process skills could be successfully taught" in that way (Nelson, Morrison, and Whitson 2015). Using a blended model, they provided scaffolded instruction at four points during the semester in order to reach students at their point of need. In this case, the librarians began the program with a quick, ten-minute visit to the students' classroom at the beginning of the semester to introduce the library and the online tutorial modules and answer any initial questions, which "sets the stage for comfortable interactions with the Librarian across the semester." Three additional points of contact, each of which was designed to meet student needs at that point in the semester, followed this initial meeting. For example, the second point of contact consisted of a "30-second welcome video" in which "the English Librarian personally welcomes students and introduces them to the *SearchPath* Tutorial." In order to adapt an earlier tutorial to the new blended model, the librarians reduced the number of concepts they covered as well as the learning activities and embedded quizzes, using them to teach students basic skills while addressing higher-order skills in later face-to-face sessions. As we have seen, limiting the number of concepts taught in any given session is more effective for face-to-face instruction and the same principle holds true in online instruction as well. In this case, the librarians used the online tutorial modules effectively to prepare students for the third point of contact, which consists of a "second face-to-face class visit." During this second class visit, the "Librarian engages students in a no-tech, hands-on learning activity, designed to develop essential critical thinking and source evaluation skills." Thus, the online tutorials prepared students to engage in higher-order information literacy skills. Since all students engaged with the same tutorial modules prior to the second face-to-face session, the librarians were able to employ those modules to establish a baseline of prior knowledge that they could then use to scaffold students up to more conceptual learning. The fourth point of contact comprised drop-in workshops that were not mandatory but were strongly encouraged by the instruction librarians during the face-to-face class visits with the promise that "if they come to the workshops with their research questions, they will leave the workshop with their research started." These workshops included only a small instructional component where librarians led a "learning activity where the student attendees work through authentic first-year English essay questions." Students then apply the strategies in this authentic exercise to their own essay questions, while the librarian provides individual help and shares "pertinent questions" with the rest of the group to build on teachable moments. In this case, online tutorials were designed to serve as one plank in a scaffolded approach to information literacy, allowing basic point-and-click instruction to take place outside of the classroom so that librarians could devote classroom time to authentic instruction of higher-order skills.

As important as point-of-need instruction is for undergraduate learning, it is even more crucial for adult and nontraditional learners since, as we know, adult learners prefer self-directed learning. With that in mind, the librarians at the University of Southern California (USC) who implemented problem-based learning within online tutorial modules also used adult learning theory to construct modules that would best promote authentic student learning. For example, the librarians applied Malcolm Knowles's theory of andragogy, which "manifests constructive learning theory through its precepts that adults be involved in their own instruction" (Halpern and Tucker 2015), which is another way of saying that adult learners prefer to have more control over their educational experience. Along with preferring self-paced instruction, adult learners also prefer instruction to "be highly relevant to assignments; be problem-based to encourage critical thinking and reflective learning; and acknowledge prior work and life experience." In this case, taking these preferences and learning styles into account, the USC librarians developed an "Information Literacy Toolkit," in which online tutorials were embedded into the curriculum by teaching faculty and instruction librarians using them as active learning tools in face-to-face instruction. Each tutorial was "aligned with the principles of adult learning theory," offering point-of-need instruction, self-paced learning, real-world problem solving, and an acknowledgment of prior work and life experience. Concentrating on social work and journalism students in particular, the library tutorials were framed within specific relevant skill sets and placed strategically throughout the curriculum, including as part of research-based course assignments. Thus, students were provided with skills-based instruction when those skills were needed to complete assignments, with, for example, "Students in the research course in the School of Social Work" completing "the Developing Keywords tutorial before the in-class library session, as they work on their first literature review assignment." In addition, the tutorials were designed so that students who had less experience conducting research could start at the beginning, while students with more experience could skip introductory material and start with the instruction they needed to direct their own learning. Most interestingly, the USC librarians designed their tutorials to acknowledge adult students' prior work and life experience, which can be a significant challenge in the asynchronous online environment. In this case, the librarians applied common scenarios that adult students might have encountered in the workplace to encourage them to reflect on their prior knowledge and apply it to library research. "For example, in the Evaluating Sources tutorial, students are asked to reflect on the

Blended Instruction	Adult Learning Theory (Andragogy)
☐ Skills-Based Tutorials	☐ Self-Directed Learning
☐ Scaffolded	☐ Real-World Problem Solving
☐ Point-of-Need Instruction	☐ Point-of-Need Instruction
☐ Student-Directed Learning	☐ Acknowledgement of Prior Work/Life Experience

Figure 5.6.   Instructional setting: Asynchronous online instruction. Jennifer S. Ferguson.

qualities of a good employee," which is then followed up later in the tutorial with an exercise that prompts them "to connect qualities of a good employee to those of a good information source." This type of exercise encourages students, both adults and traditional undergraduates, to make connections between their prior knowledge—whether from the workplace or K–12 education—with information literacy concepts and promotes both knowledge transfer and higher-order thinking. While this particular example of instructional design is framed in adult learning theory, many of those same principles, such as point-of-need instruction and engagement with prior knowledge, have been identified as important to learners at all stages of their educational experience and should be considered essential concepts to address in the development of asynchronous online tutorials.

OTHER INSTRUCTIONAL SETTINGS

While authentic methods of teaching and learning have been employed infrequently in less formal instructional settings, such as at the reference desk and during library orientations, there have been cases in which these methods were used to both enrich and assess student learning. For example, librarians at Long Island University (LIU) adapted a library orientation module called the "Amazing Library Race (ALR)" (Angell and Boss 2016) for a required one-credit first-year orientation. In this case, all students are required to take this course, which includes a single library session. This one-credit orientation introduces students to college life and "does not include a research component," focusing more on getting the students to make "connections to their peers and the institution." In order to provide interactive instruction, the ALR "directs first-year students to complete research challenges about services and resources in four different categories," with learning outcomes that focus on "providing participants with general information." As such, the "ALR does not involve librarians demonstrating or lecturing" but instead aims for the students to explore the library in a more "relaxing and entertaining" way (Angell and Boss 2016). The LIU librarians designed the ALR so that it "incorporates aspects of problem-based learning and key elements of gamification," which provides students with a primer that serves as the first scaffold in their introduction to college-level research. In this case, the librarians designed the ALR to center on "the learning needs and educational processes of students" rather than content presented by classroom instructors, allowing students to complete assigned tasks collaboratively by brainstorming a range of solutions, and then testing them. This method encouraged students to revise their solutions, as well as to learn from their peers. While the librarians are present at the beginning of the class and explain the activity, they do not provide formal instruction but instead remain present to answer questions and offer feedback. In addition, the assigned tasks "do not necessitate one overarching correct solution but rather encourage students to brainstorm unique answers using their own creativity and experiences," which engages students' prior knowledge and helps promote knowledge transfer. The ALR is structured as a kind of game that includes four tasks that students complete in groups, with the first group that completes the final task winning a prize. In this case, the LIU librarians employed gamification in a meaningful way, which involves the use of "design concepts from games and play to help people find personal connections to a real-world setting" (Nicholson 2013). Connecting information literacy concepts to real-life problem solving—making the tasks meaningful—helps connect the content that instructors want to teach with information that students need to know, making it more relevant and thus more likely to be retained.

Along with problem-based learning, librarians have also used ethnography as a pedagogy for library orientations. For example, librarians at the University of West Georgia chose to observe actual student behaviors around library use and research habits rather than relying on self-reported information from surveys, which "has often been found to be inaccurate" (Pashia and Critten 2015). In this case, the librarians note that while "the use of ethnographic methods to learn about how students authentically use the library and interact with research" has been widely adopted as a method to assess library space and services, they "seek to expand the use of ethnographic methods in libraries to support student learning through pedagogy." This pedagogical approach involves giving up a certain degree of control over student behaviors. Instead, librarians assign students a particular task—in this case, mapping the library—and then ask them to complete this task on their own while observing their methodology. While some students took shortcuts, such as copying from displayed library maps, the librarians "saw this as giving students the agency to engage with the information in the way that makes the most sense for them." The students were also asked to reflect on library spaces, how they were currently being used by the patrons they observed, and how they might use those spaces themselves. Moreover, while there was a wide variety of engagement levels, there were "many

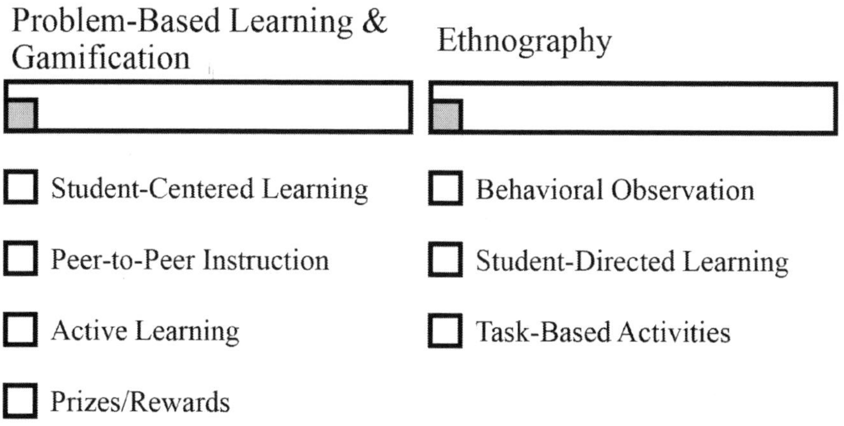

Problem-Based Learning & Gamification | Ethnography

- ☐ Student-Centered Learning
- ☐ Peer-to-Peer Instruction
- ☐ Active Learning
- ☐ Prizes/Rewards

- ☐ Behavioral Observation
- ☐ Student-Directed Learning
- ☐ Task-Based Activities

Figure 5.7. Instructional setting: Library orientation. Jennifer S. Ferguson.

students who provided thoughtful responses and demonstrated engagement by asking questions." In this case, the students were asked to play the role of ethnographer in order to "consciously observe the space and the people using it" and then synthesize what they had found. This reflection and synthesis was intended to be a starting point for introducing students to an academic library for the first time, with the expectation that their relationship to the space as well as to the research process would continue to evolve as they progressed through their education. As a result, the librarians believe that "ethnography was an especially useful framework" for designing an updated library orientation assignment "as it served as both a learning object and as an oft-used method for qualitative assessment, a site for immediate, formative feedback." This method thus included many of the aspects of authentic teaching and learning, as it employed a task-based assignment that required reflection and students received immediate feedback. Most interestingly, it also provides a framework for using ethnographic methods beyond assessing library space and services and into library instruction.

While each instructional setting poses its own pedagogical challenges, there are a great many, perhaps even unexpected, similarities involved in designing instruction around authentic teaching and learning. Almost every case study presented in this chapter includes authentic strategies that map across more than one of the common library instruction contexts. For example, while it can seem much easier to achieve authentic teaching and learning in credit-bearing courses than in other settings, one of the most common components of instructional design in credit-bearing courses, scaffolding, is also foundational for other settings including embedded librarianship and asynchronous online instruction. In addition, while one-shot sessions can prove

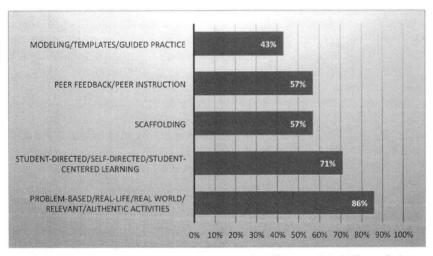

Figure 5.8. Authentic teaching in context: Proportion of cases using similar techniques.

most challenging in this area, effective instructional design for authentic teaching and learning within this context includes task-based or problem-based learning that differs more in terminology than in technique. These terms include real-life activities, real-world activities, relevant activities, and authentic activities. While the labels may differ, in each case the theory and pedagogical techniques are quite similar. As demonstrated in figure 5.8, combining these disparate labels into like-minded categories shows how common most authentic teaching strategies are across contexts. Thus, it is fairly safe to say that many characteristics of effective and authentic teaching and learning can be adapted from one instructional context to another and from one institutional context to another. Each library can employ the strategies that promote significant learning, work within specific library settings, and generate authentic assessment that can be used to demonstrate the library's value to the greater institutional mission. The next chapter will discuss how libraries can adapt authentic assessment to their individual needs in order to improve both library teaching and student learning.

REFERENCES

American Psychological Association (APA). 1997. "Learner-Centered Psychological Principles: A Framework for School Reform and Redesign." http://www.apa.org/ed/governance/bea/learner-centered.pdf.

Angell, Katelyn, and Katherine Boss. 2016. "Adapting the Amazing Library Race: Using Problem-Based Learning in Library Orientations." *College and Undergraduate Libraries* 23, no. 1 (January–March): 44–55.

Cassidy, Erin Dorris, and Kenneth E. Hendrickson. 2013. "Faculty-Librarian Micro-Level Collaboration in an Online Graduate History Course." *Journal of Academic Librarianship* 39, no. 6 (November): 458–63.

Catalano, Amy. 2015. "The Effect of a Situated Learning Environment in a Distance Education Information Literacy Course." *Journal of Academic Librarianship* 41, no. 5 (September): 653–59.

Dawe, Lydia, and Ainslie Robinson. 2017. "Wikipedia Editing and Information Literacy: A Case Study." *Information and Learning Science* 118 (1/2): 5–16.

Halpern, Rebecca, and Chimene Tucker. 2015. "Leveraging Adult Learning Theory with Online Tutorials." *Reference Services Review* 43, no. 1 (Spring): 112–24.

Hanz, Katherine, and Jessica Lange. 2013. "Using Student Questions to Direct Information Literacy Workshops." *Reference Services Review* 41, no. 3 (Fall): 532–46.

Hawes, Sandra Lee, and Jane Mason Adamson. 2016. "Flipping Out over Online Library Instruction: A Case Study in Faculty-Librarian Collaboration." *Journal of Library and Information Services in Distance Learning* 10, no. 3–4 (July–December): 254–67.

Kim, Miseon, and Michael Dolan. 2015. "'Excuse Me, but What Is a Research Paper?': Embedded Librarian Program and Information Literacy Skills of Community College Students." *Community and Junior College Libraries* 21, no. 1/2 (January–June): 53–70.

Mackey, Thomas R., and Trudi E. Jacobson. 2011. "Reframing Information Literacy as a Metaliteracy." *College and Research Libraries* 72, no. 1: (January): 62–78.

Meszaros, MaryBeth. 2010. "Who's in Charge Here? Authority, Authoritativeness, and the Undergraduate Researcher." *Communications in Information Literacy* 4, no. 1 (March): 5–11.

Nelson, Jody, Joan Morrison, and Lindsey Whitson. 2015. "Piloting a Blended Model for Sustainable IL Programming." *Reference Services Review* 43, no. 1 (February): 137–51.

Nicholson, Scott. 2013. "Meaningful Gamification: Motivating through Play instead of Manipulating through Rewards." MIT Game Lab. https://youtu.be/-zimKhhES-s.

Pashia, Angela, and Jessica Critten. 2015. "Ethnography as Pedagogy in Library Orientations." *Journal of Information Literacy* 9, no. 2 (December): 84–93.

Rahanu, Harjinder, Elli Georgiadou, Nawaz Khan, Robert Colson, Vanessa Hill, and J. Adam Edwards. 2016. "The Development of Student Learning and Information Literacy: A Case Study." *Education for Information* 32, no. 3 (July): 211–24.

Rapchak, Marcia E., Leslie A. Lewis, Julie K. Motyka, and Margaret Balmert. 2015. "Information Literacy and Adult Learners." *Adult Learning* 26, no. 4 (November): 135–42.

Roberts, Lindsay. 2017. "Research in the Real World: Improving Adult Learners Web Search and Evaluation Skills through Motivational Design and Problem-Based Learning." *College and Research Libraries* 78, no. 4 (May): 527–51.

Soules, Aline, Sarah Nielsen, Hee Youn Lee, and Kinda Al Rifae. 2013. "Embedding Information Literacy in an MA TESOL Program." *New Library World* 114, no. 1–2 (January): 32–43.

6

Adapting Authentic Assessment to Common Instructional Settings

As we have seen, authentic teaching and assessment are available to librarians working across a number of information literacy settings, from credit-bearing courses to one-shot instruction sessions. In addition, many, if not most, techniques can be adapted to each library's needs. This chapter will provide basic guidelines for adapting authentic assessment techniques to the most common instructional contexts. This chapter does not intend to provide an exhaustive list of every possible adaptation but rather will present step-by-step instructions for how each assessment instrument can be adapted to the most frequently employed instructional settings, particularly one-shot sessions, asynchronous online instruction, and library orientations. As a result, formative and summative assessment techniques that are available in most settings will receive more extensive treatment, while summative assessment techniques that have limited applicability across instructional settings will be discussed in less detail.

FORMATIVE ASSESSMENT

Discussion Boards

While implementing discussion boards is relatively simple within the context of credit-bearing courses or embedded librarianship, it can appear to be more difficult to adapt them to a more traditional one-shot session. However, based on the level of faculty-librarian collaboration, they can be successfully used in one-shot library instruction. In this case, if the librarian has a presence in a course's learning management system, even if not at the embedded level, the discussion board can be used as a forum for discussing a library assignment or for initiating a discussion of the impact that library instruction had on a student's completion of a subject-based assignment.

For example, at Simmons College, students taking a first-year writing course taught by a faculty member in nutrition receive information literacy instruction that helps them make decisions about a "best diet" for a particular population. The librarian teaches students how to research typical diets, moving from articles in the popular press to high-quality background resources to finding any scientific studies that might have been conducted around the diet. During the library instruction session, students complete a worksheet that asks them to find and evaluate each information source and then to reflect on what they found and how they might use it. As students complete the presentations on their "best diets," they are also required to post comments to the online discussion board, in which they are provided with a prompt that asks them to use the research they have conducted to highlight what makes their diet a good choice and to discuss any controversy they found in the literature that suggests it might not be the best diet. In this way, the information literacy instruction the students receive is directly related to course content, aiding in knowledge transfer, and while the students receive only one instruction session, they are prompted to continue to reflect on the quality of information they found and justify the information choices they made in arguing for their best diets. This use of a discussion board requires only that the faculty member allow the librarian to create one additional assignment—an assignment that does not require extra work by the faculty member since the librarian provides feedback on student comments. In addition, this use of a discussion board can also include a peer-to-peer component, thus adding further authentic elements to what is essentially a one-shot instruction session. At the end of the face-to-face session and online discussion, the librarian also has several assessment artifacts, including quantitative data about the students' ability to complete the library assignment, qualitative data from their written reflections, and a valuable window into the students' ability to apply the knowledge and skills gained during instruction to their subject-based assignment, which may occur a week or more after instruction. This lesson also addresses several of the ACRL information literacy frames, including: authority as constructed and contextual; information creation as a process; the value of information; and research as inquiry. Following are step-by-step instructions for implementing this type of discussion board in a one-shot session:

Step 1: Contact faculty member regarding access to course in learning management system and the addition of one discussion board assignment.

Step 2: Develop lesson plan, worksheet, and guided questions to prompt discussion.

Step 3: During instruction, focus on teaching broad concepts such as the differences in information types, which sources include which type of information, and critical evaluation of sources.

Step 4: Use worksheet as teaching tool, scaffolding students up to each source and type of information and providing hands-on practice throughout the session in order to complete each section at the appropriate point of need. Use student questions and comments as an opportunity to provide timely feedback as well as for peer instruction.

Step 5: Finish session with the written reflection and discussion of the important points learned as well as any remaining questions. Collect worksheet at the end of the class. Inform students that they will also need to post a comment on the library instruction discussion thread.

Step 6: Monitor discussion thread and provide timely feedback. Record questions and answers in order to gather additional authentic assessment data.

Guided Focus Groups and Interviews

As we have seen, this method of assessment is used most often in settings where traditional instruction and assessment are rarely employed and has proven especially useful in library orientations. In this case, librarians develop a set of questions with which to guide a discussion either after a library orientation activity, such as mapping or a scavenger hunt, or after a brief presentation by a librarian introducing students to the library's space and resources. For example, if first-year students are required to complete a library activity as part of their general orientation or within the context of the increasingly common one-credit courses that provide them with an "introduction to college life," guided focus groups and interviews can help librarians gather additional qualitative assessment data as part of this process. Even if librarians do not have classroom time in which to implement a focus group, the library activity can be designed so that students are required to participate in a guided interview by having a librarian sign off on an activity worksheet before it is handed in to the course instructor. Before signing off on the worksheet, the librarian can use the student interaction to ask a focused set of questions about the activity. For instance, if an activity requires students to locate information about the library's resources, both virtual and physical, and answer questions about what they found, the librarian who signs off on the worksheet can ask students about their experience with the activity, why they chose to highlight the resources they did, and what they still found confusing. Not only does this short interview give librarians insight into how students navigate the library and what they do or don't understand, it also offers them a chance to provide timely feedback to each student by answering any lingering questions and correcting any misperceptions. In addition, the interview serves as a qualitative supplement to the assessment data from the worksheet and provides first-year instruction librarians with valuable information about what they need to emphasize or reinforce during formal information literacy instruction. Since many, if not most, academic libraries provide basic orientations to incoming students, this technique not only offers valuable assessment data but is also relatively simple to implement. The following are step-by-step instructions for implementing this type of guided interview in a library orientation:

Sample 6.1. Worksheet with Discussion Prompts

Best Diet Worksheet

Use (library database here) to find a primary research article on your "best diet."
Your "best diet":

_____

Author(s) of article you found:

_____

Title of article you found:

_____

Title of journal in which the article was published:

_____

Publication date of the article you found:

_____

I selected this article because (for example, I found a reference to it in my
background research, it is the original research study on my diet, etc.):

_____
_____
_____

Discussion prompts: Now that you've found a variety of information sources
about your "best diet," use this space to brainstorm ideas for posting to the class
discussion board. (For example, what research have you found that makes your
"best diet" a good choice? Is there any controversy in the scholarly or popular
literature about this diet? How much evidence is there for determining whether or
not it's the "best diet"?)

_____
_____
_____
_____

Your name and email address:

_____

Do you want us to contact you for additional help?
Your question:

_____

Step 1: Design a library orientation activity worksheet that highlights the space and resources that you think are most important for first-year students to know about.

Step 2: Design three simple interview questions to ask students before signing off on the activity worksheet.

Step 3: Before signing off on the worksheet, ask students the three interview questions and code their answers.

Step 4: If possible, make a quick copy of the completed worksheet as an assessment artifact before handing it back to the student. If it's not possible to make a copy of the worksheet, make a note of whether the assignment was completed correctly or incorrectly, and keep track of the number of students in each category.

Step 5: Share assessment data from the worksheets and interviews with first-year instruction librarians.

Minute Papers

Minute papers are one of the easiest assessment instruments to implement in any instructional setting. They take very little time to complete and can be a most convenient assessment in a one-shot session that lasts for sixty minutes or less. However, as they are usually designed, minute papers rarely qualify as authentic assessments, since most of them more closely resemble the guided interview questions noted earlier and don't require students to synthesize, analyze, or apply their knowledge. In addition, minute papers that do not require students to enact their knowledge but instead function as a self-assessment tell us very little about what students actually learned. Thus, to be an effective assessment instrument, minute papers need to include at least one short task and a brief evaluation or reflection on that task, both of which directly relate to the content just taught. For example, in a typical one-shot instruction session for a first-year writing class, students are introduced to the array of information resources that libraries provide to support their academic work. They are generally taught what those resources are, the types of information they contain, how that information is used to construct an argument, and how to evaluate information for authority, credibility, and bias. Even within the context of a session that lasts for sixty minutes or less or an introductory session in a tiered information literacy program, students are generally provided with hands-on practice in searching a variety of library and web resources and evaluating their content. In this type of session, librarians can ask students to find at least one source they might use in an upcoming assignment and can provide them with a framework for thinking about why they might choose one resource over another, providing guiding questions, such as "Does the resource provide valuable statistics? key historical context? new information?" or other criteria. Toward the end of the lesson, the librarian can distribute a minute paper that asks students to cite the resource they found—whether it's an article or a website, and then answer a question about the resource they selected. In this case,

Sample 6.2a. Library Orientation Assignment

Name: _____ Date: _____

Let's get started! First, find the library on Instagram (or Facebook or Twitter, if you prefer). Follow the library; then have a look at a few posts. Find a post that you find interesting and tell us why it's interesting and how you might use it. (For example, it provides updated hours or highlights an interesting resource or topic.)

_____
_____
_____
_____

Next, start at the library's website (library URL here).

What are three ways you can contact a librarian?

     1. _____
     2. _____
     3. _____

Think of a course you're taking this semester (or a course you want to take soon). Find a research guide on the library's website that is related to that course or subject.

     What is the URL for the guide? _____
     Who is the librarian that you would contact for help in this subject area?
     _____

Search the library catalog for a book on a topic you're interested in.

     Is the book available, or does it have another status (e.g., online, due, lib use only)? _____
     What is the title? _____
     What is the location (e.g., "Reserves" or "Book Stacks")? _____
     What is the call number? _____

Find an available book and bring it to the research help desk.

Tell the librarian at the research help desk why you chose that book and how you found it. Then ask the librarian to initial below!

Librarian's initials: _____

Date: _____

Sample 6.2b. Guided Interview Questions and Coding Sheet

Sample Guided Interview Questions

What is the most useful thing you learned about the library?

Why did you choose to highlight that space, service, or resource?

What do you still find confusing about the library?

Sample Codes

Most useful: (library space/library website/specific resource)

Highlighted area: (personally interesting/useful for a class)

Most confusing: (library space/library website/specific resource)

Coding Sheet (check each category that applies for each student:)

	Library Space	Library Website	Specific Resource	Personally Interesting	Useful for a Class
What is the most useful thing you learned about the library?					
Why did you choose to highlight that resource or service?					
What do you still find confusing about the library?					

students who chose to cite an article can be asked to reflect on what type of article they found, scholarly or popular, as well as what differentiates the two. If the resource they selected is a website, students can be asked to reflect on what makes that website suitable for academic work. After they complete the brief task and reflection, they are also provided with space to ask any additional lingering questions they might have. Students provide their name and email address and hand the paper in at the end of the session, which allows the teaching librarian to assess their ability to perform the task as well as their ability to evaluate the information they found. In addition, if there is time toward the end of the session, the librarian can anonymously share some of the lingering questions, especially those that appear on more than one paper, and provide timely feedback. If there isn't time at the end of the session, the librarian can email the students with answers to their questions and/or to correct any mistakes they made in either evaluating or citing their selected resources. Not only is this type of minute paper easy to implement in a brief amount of time, it also asks students to synthesize, analyze, and apply their knowledge, making it more authentic than the typical self-evaluation. In addition, this type of assessment can also help improve instruction if students continually find it difficult to identify an appropriate resource or to understand what makes one resource better than another for academic work, thus providing librarians with both an assessment of student learning and a glimpse into teaching effectiveness. This one brief instrument can then serve two purposes when reporting out to stakeholders—demonstrating the library's commitment both to student learning and to continuous instructional improvement. Following are step-by-step instructions for implementing this type of minute paper in a sixty-minute one-shot session:

Step 1: Design a minute paper that asks sudents to perform one task related to an essential learning outcome and then reflect on it. Leave space for students to ask additional questions and have them provide their name and email address for librarian responses.

Step 2: Design the instruction session so students understand how to search library resources and that provides a framework for them to evaluate the resources they find, no matter where they find them.

Step 3: Concentrate on teaching students a few broad concepts, and allow time for hands-on practice.

Step 4: Distribute the minute paper at the end of the session. Leave approximately five to ten minutes for students to complete them.

Step 5: Have students hand in the minute paper when completed. If time allows, anonymously share common lingering questions with the class and answer those questions.

Step 6: Assess the minute papers for both the students' ability to complete the task and their ability to evaluate sources.

Step 7: Email students with timely feedback to their questions (if they weren't answered during class) and to correct any mistakes or misperceptions.

Sample 6.3. Minute Paper

Please complete the task and answer one of the two questions:

1. Write the citation information for one resource that you found during this session.

_____

_____

_____

_____

2. If the resource you found is an article, how can you tell if it is from a scholarly or popular source?

_____

_____

_____

_____

3. If the resource you found was a website, how can you tell if it is appropriate for academic work?

_____

_____

_____

_____

Your name and email address:

_____

_____

Do you have any further questions that you would like a librarian to answer?

_____

_____

_____

_____

Step 8: Revise instruction based on tasks or concepts students continue to struggle with.

Peer Evaluation

As we have seen, peer instruction and peer evaluation are powerful teaching and assessment tools. In addition, since first-year students in particular have trouble asking for help from a librarian (Head 2013) and students at every level often turn to their peers and family members before asking a librarian for help (Thomas, Tewell, and Willson 2017), incorporating peer evaluation into assessment can alleviate some of the insecurity students feel both with seeking help and with reflecting on the performance of specific tasks. Providing feedback to their peers also helps students better understand a topic or task, encouraging higher-order thinking. Thus, adding a peer evaluation component to library instruction can both enhance student learning and provide teaching librarians with an additional assessment instrument. Moreover, peer evaluation can be incorporated into almost any instructional setting, from including it in discussion board assignments for credit-bearing classes to using it as part of a problem-based active learning exercise in a one-shot session. For example, an instruction session can be designed so that the librarian spends the first half of the class providing instruction that focuses on a few major concepts and then divides the class into groups to solve a relevant information problem. Each group has a fixed amount of time to solve the problem and write a brief reflection on how they solved it. At the end of this task, each group exchanges their solution with the group closest to them. Each group then provides feedback on the other group's solution, comparing and contrasting their peers' solution with their own. Once each group completes both processes, the peer evaluation sheets are turned in to the librarian, who then initiates a brief discussion about the process of solving the problem and the challenges each group faced, both with providing a solution and with offering peer feedback, encouraging students to share what they learned about both and correcting any common mistakes or misperceptions. This type of peer evaluation exercise includes all the components of authentic assessment as well as promoting higher-order thinking skills and is similar to a minute paper in that it provides a glimpse into teaching effectiveness and can be used to help improve instruction if the students consistently find it difficult to solve the assigned problem or have a hard time evaluating their peers. Following are step-by-step instructions for implementing this type of peer evaluation in a single instruction session in any setting:

Step 1: Develop a relevant information problem that a small group can solve in a relatively short amount of time. Design a worksheet that lists the problem, provides space for a solution and a reflection on the process, and includes a section for peer feedback.

Step 2: Design an instruction session that focuses on a few broad concepts during the first half of the class and allows time for students to solve problems, provide feedback, and discuss the results during the second half of the session.

Step 3: Divide the class into small groups of three or four students (based on the number of students in the class) and distribute the peer evaluation worksheet during the second half of the session. Give each group a specific letter designation to include on their worksheet (group A, B, etc.).

Step 4: Explain both the problem-solving and peer evaluation components. Allow approximately ten to fifteen minutes for both processes based on the length of the session.

Step 5: Have students hand in the peer evaluation worksheets when completed. Initiate discussion using group designations, asking specific questions about how each group solved the problem, such as "Why did your group choose to use the resource you did? Was it easy/hard to solve the problem using that resource?" Correct any common student mistakes or misperceptions.

Step 6: Assess the peer evaluation worksheets for both the students' ability to solve the problem and the quality of the feedback they provided to their peers.

Step 7: Revise instruction based on tasks or concepts students continue to struggle with.

Performative Task-Based Assignments

Performative task-based assignments are another authentic assessment that can be easily implemented across almost every instructional setting. Whether they are used as scaffolded exercises across one or more sections of an embedded librarian program or as a teaching and learning artifact in a one-shot session, well-designed performative task-based assignments can incorporate nearly every element of authentic assessment and provide teaching librarians with a measure of both student learning and teaching effectiveness. For example, librarians can design a task-based worksheet that enables scaffolding within the one-shot session itself, with students moving through increasingly difficult tasks as the class progresses. A lesson designed in this way engages with students' prior knowledge and focuses on teaching broad concepts, starting with the basics of identifying keywords and using those keywords to find reliable background information. In this case, the librarian might start the class by asking students how they normally conduct their research, emphasizing that there are no wrong answers. Since the answer to that question is generally that they start by searching Google and find Wikipedia useful, the librarian then has the opportunity to connect sources like Wikipedia to library reference resources, explaining what kind of information Wikipedia contains and why they find it useful but also why they are generally not allowed to cite it. This lesson starts by validating their prior process, teaching them to begin evaluating the sources they discover, and leading them to more reliable providers of the background information they find so useful. At the beginning of the class, the librarian hands out a task-based worksheet and students are asked to flip it over, using the blank side of the sheet to begin with a keyword exercise. In this case, students write their topic on the blank page. It should also be emphasized that, whether employing the blank side of a worksheet or a separate piece of paper or index card for this exercise, given the strong connection between handwriting and memory, it is important that students complete these tasks by hand (Mueller and Oppenheimer 2014). After they have their topics written down, the librarian demonstrates how to take a topic or research question and turn it into a keyword search. Once keywords are demonstrated, the librarian briefly demonstrates how to search a reference resource using the keywords first identified, then how to use a reference entry on a particular topic to add additional keywords

Sample 6.4. Peer Evaluation Worksheet

Group Name/Number:

1. Problem:

2. Your group's solution:

3. Why did your group choose this solution?

Peer Evaluation Section

Evaluating Group's Name/Number: _____

1. Was your group's solution to the problem the same or different than this one?

2. If your solution was the same, did you choose that solution for the same reason? Why or why not? If your solution was different, what do you think about the strengths or weaknesses of the above solution?

and concepts. Students then search the reference resource to find an entry on their topic. Once they find an entry, they take a few minutes to read it and to identify additional keywords to add to their list. Once students complete this brief exercise, the librarian then demonstrates a more advanced search interface such as a typical journal database or discovery layer. For first-year students, the discovery layer may prove more valuable, while for more advanced students a subject-specific database might be more appropriate. In both cases, the difference in information types as well as levels of authority in scholarly versus popular sources should be explained so that students are equipped to judge which resource might be most appropriate for their purpose. After a brief demonstration of how keywords can be combined into an effective search strategy in order to find books and journal articles, the students are asked to flip the worksheet over and complete the first task using the keywords they identified in the first part of the class along with the search strategies that the librarian demonstrated. This particular task should be relevant to the specific class, and its completion should result in students finding a source that they can use in an upcoming assignment. Connecting these strategies directly to the requirements of their assignment aids in knowledge transfer, helping students link the library lesson to class content.

As students complete each task, a librarian can provide instant feedback before progressing to the next task, spending time roaming while students complete the tasks and using the obstacles students encounter or questions they ask to correct any mistakes or misperceptions and reinforce the content of the lesson. In addition, when students ask really good questions or discover something on their own, these insights can be shared with the rest of the class as a form of peer teaching. In this case, the performative task-based assignment functions as both a learning tool and an authentic assessment instrument, driving student engagement with the material and asking them to apply their knowledge in order to measure essential learning outcomes. It also scaffolds students through increasingly difficult tasks throughout the course of the session. In addition, if the final task on the worksheet includes a reflection or search log component, the entire exercise will include all of the attributes of authentic assessment and can be completed within a relatively short time. Ideally, the reflection should ask them to circle back to the beginning of the class to close the loop between their prior knowledge and search strategy and compare it with what they learned during the instruction session. Not only does this type of performative task-based assignment act as an authentic teaching and learning tool but it also provides librarians with both quantitative (what can students do) and qualitative (what do students think) assessment data, which can be used longitudinally to report out to stakeholders as well as internally to improve lesson planning and teaching effectiveness. Demonstrated improvement in both student learning and librarian teaching over time can tell a powerful story about the library's commitment to students' academic success. Following are step-by-step instructions for implementing this type of performative task-based assignment into a single instruction session in any setting:

Step 1: Develop learning outcomes (what students should be able to do) relevant to the class assignment and design a worksheet that asks students to perform tasks related to that learning outcome. (For example, faculty might require that students use at least one to three scholarly sources for their papers. In this case, you would design a task that allows the students to come away with at least one scholarly source as well as the ability to find additional scholarly sources on their own.) This worksheet should require students to complete a set of tasks, document the process they used, and reflect on what they did or did not do and why.

Step 2: Design an instruction session that scaffolds students through increasingly complex tasks, using each task to build on and reinforce the prior task. Focus on teaching students broad concepts, such as the differences between types of information and how to evaluate sources for quality and reliability.

Step 3: Allot most of the session time to hands-on practice and discussion, roaming as students complete each task and using questions and obstacles to provide immediate feedback as well as librarian- and peer-teaching moments.

Step 4: Have students hand in the worksheets when completed. If time allows, close the loop by initiating a discussion comparing and contrasting students' prior information-seeking behavior with the lessons learned during the library session.

Step 5: Assess the performative task-based worksheets for the students' ability to complete the tasks and their reflections on what they learned.

Step 6: Email students with additional feedback to correct their mistakes or misperceptions or to answer any lingering questions.

Step 7: Revise instruction based on common tasks or concepts with which students continue to struggle.

Problem-Based Activities

Problem-based activities function very similarly to performative task-based assignments but in some ways are more easily scalable for large classes. In addition, they can be very useful in an active learning environment where students work together to solve common information problems, whether for specific classes and assignments or within the context of lifelong learning for their professions. In this case, librarians would identify an information problem relevant to a particular course such as locating reliable information that will help business students identify the strengths, weaknesses, opportunities, and threats specific to a particular company or industry in order to complete an assignment for a class on organizational behavior. Large undergraduate class sizes are common in many academic disciplines, particularly those focused on professional preparation such as business and the health sciences. Since these classes are often held in lecture halls and the number of students in each section usually exceeds the capacity of library classrooms or other computer labs, library instruction tends to take place in the students' regular classroom. Thus, problem-

Sample 6.5. Performative Task-Based Worksheet

Use (a library database) to find a scholarly journal article on your topic:

_____

Author(s) of article

_____

Title of article

_____

Title of journal in which the article was published

_____

Date article was published

_____

I selected this article because (for example, it provides important historical context, adds new information, supports my argument, includes key statistics, etc.):

_____

_____

Now search Google for the same topic. How does using the library database compare to Google? (For example, was it easier or harder to find a full-text scholarly article on your topic in one or the other? What are the advantages or disadvantages of each? Which would you search first and why?)

_____

_____

_____

_____

_____

Your name and email address

_____

Do you want us to contact you for additional help?

Your question(s):

_____

_____

based group learning may be the best way to enact authentic teaching and learning in this setting, particularly in the context of a flipped classroom or one-shot model. For example, depending on the level of faculty-librarian collaboration, it might be relatively easy to employ the flipped classroom model in which asynchronous online tutorials are combined with an instruction session. In this case, students can be provided with a link to one or more asynchronous online tutorials in their learning management course page. They are asked to complete the tutorial(s) prior to the librarian's visit to their classroom. This tutorial might include a simple quiz that can help the librarian understand the short-term skills students seem to have mastered, as well as the areas in which they continue to struggle. Using the information gathered from the tutorials, the librarian can design a problem-based activity that is based on the skills the students should already have but challenges them to solve a more complex information challenge than they might have encountered in the quiz.

The librarian begins the class with a brief review of the tutorial content and answers any lingering questions students might have about it. The students are then divided into groups, with the librarian assigning the information problem and handing out a worksheet on which each group records their solution to the problem along with their reasons for solving the problem in the way that they did. The information problem should be common to the subject discipline and, ideally, related to the real-world problems students will need to solve within their professions. For example, students studying business often have to research companies and identify salient points about them, including finding current analyses of the strengths, weaknesses, opportunities, and threats (SWOT) they face. The librarian could then identify a large public company and ask the students to find reliable SWOT data on that company. To make the problem even more relevant to a real-world task, the students might be required to find credible information without the use of library databases, since many, if not most, of the students will not have access to those databases in the workplace. Once each group solves the problem, they designate a spokesperson to report out on the group's solution. The librarian then provides feedback and encourages class discussion around each solution. At the end of the session, the librarian collects the worksheets to use as authentic assessment artifacts. This type of problem-based lesson includes a task-based activity, immediate feedback, peer learning, and a reflection component, which makes authentic assessment available to librarians teaching large classes. In addition, this method can be employed even if students don't complete online tutorials prior to class. Instead, the librarian can provide brief instruction at the beginning of class and then divide the students into problem-solving groups, roaming the room as the groups work on the problem in order to answer questions or to provide immediate feedback. The real-world nature of the problem-solving activity encourages knowledge transfer, directly connecting information literacy with workplace needs. This type of authentic exercise can also be used to demonstrate the library's value to stakeholders who report to accrediting bodies and funding agencies on student career readiness. Following are step-by-step instructions for implementing this type of problem-based activity into a single instruction session in any setting:

Step 1: Develop an information problem relevant to the real-world information needs of a subject-based discipline. Create a worksheet that groups can use to record both their solution to the problem and their reasoning.

Step 2: If using the flipped classroom model, talk to faculty about embedding a link to online tutorials on the course's learning management page. Develop tutorials that explain key concepts that students need to understand in order to solve their problems. These tutorials might focus on one area, such as how to find and evaluate sources outside of the library context, and might include an embedded quiz.

Step 3: Start the session with a brief review of tutorial content, especially focusing on any concepts the students seemed to struggle with frequently. If not using the flipped classroom model, start the session with relatively brief instruction that focuses on the key concepts—not more than two—that students will need to understand in order to solve the problem.

Step 4: Divide the students into groups and provide each group with a worksheet. Describe the information problem to the class and roam the room while students work in groups to solve the problem. Allow a fixed amount of time—approximately twenty minutes in a sixty-minute session for the groups to work on the problem.

Step 5: At the end of the allotted time, ask each group to report out on their solution to the problem. Provide feedback and correct any misunderstandings. Once all groups have reported out, initiate discussion on the nature of the problem, the solutions students found, and what worked or didn't work for them.

Step 6: At the end of the session, collect the worksheets to use both as authentic assessment artifacts and as tools to help teaching librarians revise instruction based on common tasks or concepts with which students continue to struggle.

Quizzes

As we have seen, while quizzes are the most common assessment instrument used by instruction librarians, fixed-answer quizzes rarely qualify as authentic assessments. However, with some modification, quizzes can provide authentic assessment data, which is especially helpful in asynchronous online instruction, where opportunities for authentic teaching and learning are more difficult to create. In this case, depending on the software to which librarians have access, a quiz can be constructed not only to include fixed-answer questions but also to require students to perform specific tasks and answer questions about their performance of those tasks. This type of short-answer format can also include a brief reflection component that requires students to think about the choices they make, activating metacognition. For example, librarians who exclusively provide introductory information literacy instruc-

---

Sample 6.6. Problem-Based Activity Worksheet

Problem statement (Sample: Find reliable information on the strengths, weaknesses, opportunities, and threats facing company X, and answer the questions below.)

What did you find, where did you find it, and how do you know it's reliable?

_____
_____
_____
_____
_____
_____
_____
_____
_____
_____
_____

What strategies did you use to find that information and why did you choose that approach?

_____
_____
_____
_____
_____
_____
_____
_____
_____
_____
_____

---

tion in an asynchronous online format (as opposed to a flipped classroom model in which tutorial modules are completed before face-to-face instruction) may want to develop modules in which students are required to complete specific tasks such as evaluating an information source or finding a particular type of information, answer a multiple-choice question, then reflect on both the task and their answer using an open response box. Open source tutorial software such as Guide on the Side (GotS) uses a split-screen model to include more authenticity and active learning than typical screencast tutorials. and it can be configured so that students are required to complete specific tasks and answer multiple-choice questions before proceeding to the next screen. In addition, GotS includes the ability to add a free response box that provides students with "an opportunity to reflect more deeply on their learning process" (University of Arizona Libraries 2017). Interestingly, GotS tutorials can "also combine formative and summative assessment in a single tutorial," since the platform can calculate "last-submitted responses to questions embedded in the main tutorial" as well as "attach a 'quiz' at the end that calculates first-submitted responses" (Sherriff 2017). Since this platform offers the option to design both fixed response and open response questions, it is possible to create authentic quizzes that also include a learning artifact—in this case a certificate "that records a learner's correct responses, incorrect responses, free responses, overall scores, and a timestamp"—that the student can email directly to the librarian or the faculty member for feedback.

In addition to GotS, Springshare has also recently introduced a split-screen tutorial platform called LibWizard, which includes some, though not all, of the same functionality (see Sherriff for a thorough overview of GotS and LibWizard). This type of tutorial provides a number of advantages for authentic teaching and learning since it can be configured to provide immediate feedback on individual answers, encourage iterative learning, and prompt students to reflect on both the process and their learning. In addition, GotS tutorials can be used to introduce students to the hands-on nature of searching for and retrieving information as well as the more evaluative nature of information literacy. This last concept is especially important when students have assignments that require them, for example, to differentiate between qualitative and quantitative research articles or to find authoritative information sources on a particular topic and explain what gives those sources authority. The formative and summative capabilities of GotS also allow librarians to compare students' answers (which they can revise) during the tutorial with their answers on the final quiz (which they cannot revise), enabling teaching librarians to gain a better understanding of both student learning and the tutorial's effectiveness. For example, if students are able to revise their answers throughout the tutorial but still get the answers wrong on the final quiz, it may mean that the helper text explaining the tasks is not well designed, or it might be that students need more extensive help understanding particular concepts than previously understood. Thus, librarians could address the misunderstandings by providing feedback on the students' certificates and rethink issues of instructional design or concept emphasis. These certificates could then be used both to assess student learning and help encourage improvements in online teaching. Following are step-by-step instructions for implementing this type of authentic quiz in asynchronous online split-screen tutorials as well as sample authentic quiz questions that could be used in any instructional setting:

Step 1: Develop at least one learning outcome (what students should be able to do) relevant to a class assignment, an introductory session, or a subject-based discipline. (For example, faculty might want students to find two or three research articles and identify the type of research represented, such as qualitative or quantitative research in the health sciences.)

Step 2: Choose an appropriate resource, such as the CINAHL database, that would help students complete the assignment. Design a tutorial to include instructions relevant to the class assignment and resource being used.

Step 3: Design tasks that the student needs to perform in order to use the resource effectively and complete the quiz. (For example, start by providing instructions for how to get started searching the database, how to identify parts of a record, and how to use the record to identify qualitative and quantitative research.)

Step 4: After students have been instructed in how to search and evaluate, design a task that they need to perform in order to answer the quiz questions. For example, have students search the database for two specific articles that represent good examples of quantitative and qualitative research and then answer questions about those articles. If students select the wrong answer, they should be prompted with the correct answer and allowed to change their initial response.

Step 5: After each task and fixed-answer question is completed, ask an open-response question related to the task such as "Was it easy to identify the type of research reported in this article? Why or why not? How could you tell?"

Step 6: After fixed-answer and open-response questions are completed, provide a review of the material covered in the tutorial, walking students through searching the database and finding key information in the article record.

Step 7: At the end of the review, have students complete a final quiz in which they are not allowed to change their answers. Include an open-response box for further questions or comments. Have students email a certificate of completion to the librarian.

Step 8: Review student certificates to assess student learning and to revise the tutorial if necessary. Provide feedback to students as appropriate. Share information from the certificate with interested faculty members.

Reflections

Used as standalone assessments or included as a section of a larger assessment such as a task-based worksheet or authentic quiz, reflections are a powerful learning tool, since they require students to think about their own thinking. Reflections can also be used in any instructional setting, whether as one assessment among many in a credit-bearing course, as part of an asynchronous online tutorial, at the end of a one-shot session, or as a final assessment within a tiered information literacy program. The key to implementing an authentic reflection is to require students to reflect on something they have done in class rather than to assess their own abilities. For example, minute papers are often considered reflections since they usually ask students to list one thing they learned in class, one thing they're still confused about, and one thing they still don't understand. However, students aren't always the best judges of their own learning or even of what it was important to take away from an instruction session. Depending on the teaching librarian, students may describe something they learned—but the thing they learned wasn't actually one of the important learning outcomes for the class. For instance, if a key student learning outcome for an instruction session is for students to understand how to evaluate different types of scholarly literature but a student says that the one thing they learned was how to access the

---

Sample 6.7. Quiz Questions

First Question Sequence

Search (name of database) to find the article titled (article title here).

In what journal was the article published? (multiple choice)

When was the article published? (multiple choice)

What type of research does this article describe? (multiple choice: quantitative, qualitative, literature review, meta-analysis)

Was it easy to identify the type of research reported in this article? Why or why not? How could you tell? (free response)

Second Question Sequence

Same as first question sequence but using a different article with a different research methodology to test their evaluative abilities.

Final Quiz

Search (name of database) to find the article titled (use a different article with a different research methodology).

In what journal was the article published? (multiple choice)

When was the article published? (multiple choice)

Does this article report original quantitative or qualitative research, or is it a review of the literature? (multiple choice)

Was it easy to identify the type of research reported in this article? Why or why not? How could you tell? (free response)

---

library's website, then the student learning goal for this session may not have been met—at least for this student. Indeed, in this case there is no way to know whether or not the student learned to evaluate information at all. Thus this type of reflection is not an authentic assessment of student learning but rather an assessment of what students thought they learned, which is a very different concept. Moreover, while this type of reflection might be useful to teaching librarians in order to help improve their practice, there is no guarantee that the students didn't learn what they needed to learn; they might have just written what was easiest and quickest or what first came to mind and was easy to explain, which wouldn't have much value in either case.

However, reflections can be implemented to encourage students to think and write about specific learning outcomes as opposed to their thoughts and feelings. In this case, the reflection would ask students to answer questions about tasks they performed and the processes they used to perform them, prompting them to be specific and provide examples. For example, a reflection might require a student to answer a question about how their research process changed over the course of a semester or academic year, why they chose to cite specific resources, or what makes one resource better than another for their individual research. In addition, this type of reflection can be done individually or in groups, with large classes or small. In a large class, groups might work together on a problem-based activity and then reflect on their solution to the problem and share it with the class. In a smaller class or one-shot session, students might be encouraged to reflect on what they learned and be encouraged to provide specific examples of how they might conduct research going forward and why. This type of reflection prompts students to examine their own processes and exercise higher-order thinking skills. In both situations—whether in a large class working on a problem-based activity or in a smaller one-shot session—a reflection would add an additional authentic component that provides librarians with more powerful assessment data than with a task-based assignment or problem-based activity alone, not only allowing librarians to observe a student's ability to solve a research problem but also to encourage students to think more deeply about how and why they chose a particular process or solution, providing instructors with insight into their thinking that can be used both to assess their grasp of specific concepts as well as our ability to teach them. Following are step-by-step instructions for implementing this type of reflection as part of a problem-based activity or task-based assignment in any setting:

Step 1: Follow the initial steps for implementing a problem-based activity or performative task-based assignment, including designing a session, creating a task-based worksheet, or developing a problem-based activity.

Step 2: Design a reflection using prompts related to the task or activity that students performed during the session.

Step 3: Once the task has been completed or the activity reported out, have students complete the reflection. Include from one to three prompts, depending on the length of the class.

Step 4: Have students hand in the reflection when completed. If time allows, close the loop by initiating a discussion regarding what students thought about the task or activity.

Step 5: Assess the reflections for students' grasp of higher-order concepts, ability to incorporate what they learned, and whether or not what they thought was important actually matched the class learning outcomes.

Sample 6.8. Reflection Prompts

Describe the process you used to (solve the problem or complete the task) during this class. Why did you choose to (solve the problem or complete the task) the way you did?

Will your process for doing academic research change now that you've had library instruction? Why or why not? Please be specific and give examples.

Do you think learning more about the research process in this class will help you in your other classes? Why or why not? Please be specific and give examples.

Step 6: Revise instruction based on common misperceptions, misunderstandings, or concepts with which students continue to struggle.

SUMMATIVE ASSESSMENT

Since many authentic summative assessment techniques are relatively inaccessible to librarians working outside of credit-bearing information literacy classes or extensive embedded librarianship, and because these techniques have received a great deal of attention in the library literature already, this section will focus on explaining how librarians might conceive of implementing them within more common instructional settings such as one-shot sessions and asynchronous online instruction. As a result, some techniques will include step-by-step instructions for adapting them to common settings, while in other cases suggestions for supplementing formative assessment with additional assessment instruments will be provided. Given that it is often difficult to differentiate between the impact of library instruction and discipline-based classroom instruction on summative assessments like annotated bibliographies and research papers, these instruments may instead be used to add additional assessment data to that gathered from more easily implemented formative assessments.

Annotated Bibliographies

The use of annotated bibliographies as summative assessment instruments has been widely discussed in the pedagogical literature of higher education as well as in the library literature. Because annotated bibliographies require students to enact their learning, they can be a highly effective tool for assessing whether or not students understand how to search for information, how to choose appropriate sources, how to evaluate those sources, and how to incorporate information sources into their knowledge base in order to make a larger point or to create new knowledge. However, if students attend one library instruction session toward the beginning of the semester or are exposed only to a set of asynchronous online tutorials, it can be difficult, if not impossible, to make the case that library instruction had a strong impact on their annotated bibliographies, especially if there is a wide gap in time between the library class and an assignment's due date. Thus, analyzing annotated bibliographies is almost pointless as a standalone assessment for one-shot library instruction. However, annotated bibliographies can be an extremely useful supplement to earlier, formative assessment. For example, if during a one-shot session a teaching librarian implements an authentic assessment and collects an artifact of that assessment such as a worksheet or authentic minute paper, then those formative instruments can be compared with students' annotated bibliographies to obtain a clearer picture of the development of students' skills and abilities throughout the semester. If the formative assessment includes a reflection component, it can be interesting to see whether or not students apply what they learned to a graded assignment, which would provide evidence of knowledge transfer. For example, if in a reflection a student indicates that he or she understand the differences between scholarly and popular sources of information but fails to apply that understanding to an assignment that requires the use of scholarly sources only, then that student is clearly struggling with a key concept and with transferring knowledge from the instruction session to a discipline-based assignment. Identifying this type of performance gap can help librarians not only understand when instruction needs to take place vis-à-vis student point of need, but can also help librarians identify concepts that need further emphasis during information literacy instruction. For example, if students make the same or similar mistakes in a large percentage of the annotated bibliographies, those bibliographies would provide additional signs of student learning or misunderstanding, providing teaching librarians with further evidence of the need for increased library instruction to share with faculty and other stakeholders. Moreover, if students seem to have retained the concepts taught during library instruction, the annotated bibliographies can serve as examples of teaching effectiveness and library impact, which can also be shared to demonstrate the library's commitment to student learning outcomes. In both cases, annotated bibliographies can supplement authentic formative assessment in order both to assess student learning and teaching effectiveness and to advocate for an increased library presence and demonstrate the impact of information literacy instruction.

Portfolios

Like annotated bibliographies, portfolios that include learning artifacts based only on library instruction are difficult to implement outside of credit-bearing information literacy classes or fully embedded librarianship. However, if librarians teaching in more traditional instructional settings can arrange for access to student portfolios, they can then be used in much the same way as other summative assessments such as annotated bibliographies. In this case, portfolios can be especially useful because they usually contain multiple graded assignments that can demonstrate student progress throughout the semester. Thus comparing formative assessment instruments focused on information literacy with student progress as demonstrated by a portfolio can help librarians identify when and how they might work with students who may be falling behind, reaching them at their point of need rather than afterward. In this case, collaboration with a faculty member is the key, both for accessing the portfolios and for intervening when students need help with finding, evaluating, and using information sources. A strong relationship with the faculty member could result in teaching librarians' providing additional formal instruction or in students being referred to the librarian for follow-up help. In this case, the teaching librarian would periodically assess the learning artifacts in the student portfolios and contact the faculty member if many students appeared to be struggling with the same concepts, such as finding information sources appropriate to their assignments or understanding the difference between types of information. At that point, the faculty member could refer the students for a mandatory individual appointment with a librarian, or the librarian could offer times for students to sign up to work in small groups, which would minimize the impact that individual follow-up appointments might have on the librarian's workload. For example, in a small-group setting the librarian could initiate a discussion of the key concept that most students are struggling with, such as identifying appropriate information sources for a specific assignment. In this case, the librarian might prepare a set of questions to begin a conversation around source evaluation. Based on student responses, the librarian might then focus on reinforcing a particular point, such as how to use clues such as the title of a journal, the length of an article, and the structure of that article in order to help students learn to tell the difference between scholarly and popular articles no matter where they find them. In addition, students—especially first-year students—often use inappropriate sources because of the difficulty they have with choosing from the vastly increased and increasingly complex array of resources that they encounter in academic libraries. Feeling overwhelmed, they may continue to use the methods that served them well enough in high school, relying "on their deeply ingrained habit of using Google searches and Wikipedia" (Head 2013), which was often adequate for high school papers. Thus, access to portfolios as well as follow-up instruction can help identify student sticking points and help intervene at their point of need and before they receive a final, and perhaps discouraging, grade. This type of support can help not only to reinforce and improve student learning but also to demonstrate the library's commitment to a student-centered approach, which affirms the library's centrality to teaching and learning and its capacity to assist with pressing institutional issues such as enrollment and retention (Bell 2008).

Pre-/Post-Tests

Pre-/post-tests are a form of summative assessment that can be implemented in the most common instructional settings, including one-shot sessions, embedded librarianship, and asynchronous online instruction. For example, as we have seen, many instructional technologies such as Guide on the Side and LibWizard, as well as more traditional video tutorial platforms, provide fairly robust quizzing and testing capabilities. The most difficult aspect of implementing pre-/post-tests is in constructing an authentic testing instrument. While it is relatively simple to design multiple-choice and true-false tests and quizzes, authentic tests can be more challenging both to design and to assess. In addition, without a degree of faculty cooperation, pre-/post-tests can be difficult to implement in one-shot sessions. That said, if there is a strong faculty-librarian relationship, pre-tests can be administered as take-home assignments during the first or second class session, which can be especially useful in upper-level subject-based classes in which students will need to master specific resources in order to complete their assignments. For example, nursing students need to understand the foundations of evidence-based medicine in order to incorporate it into their professional practice as nurses. One part of mastering the concepts inherent to evidence-based medicine is to understand how nursing research is conducted, including learning how to search databases for research articles in order to create a literature review that synthesizes original research and draws conclusions from it. To conduct that type of research, nursing students need to master databases such as CINAHL and Medline, constructing keyword and subject searches in order to find articles that meet a specific set of criteria. Many upper-level nursing research classes design their assignments to ensure that students acquire these skills and often incorporate library instruction into their classes. In this case, the librarian and faculty member agree in advance on a set of library learning outcomes and design a pre-/post-test instrument that measures students' progress before and after the instruction session. The faculty member provides students with a pre-test take-home assignment, ideally after the first regular class session, which they complete and return for scoring by the librarian. Because this assignment does not take away any class time or impose an additional grading burden on the faculty member, implementing this type of pre-test should be fairly straightforward. After scoring the pre-tests, the librarian has the added advantage of gaining a greater understanding of the students' prior knowledge and can then design an instruction session that addresses gaps in students' knowledge and corrects any misunderstandings they may have. At the end of the instruction session, the librarian administers the post-test to assess any differences between students' initial answers and their answers after library instruction, which assesses both student learning and teaching effectiveness. In addition, since a take-home pre-test allows students to revise or correct their answers before scoring, a post-test in which students are unable to correct or revise their answers offers powerful evidence of whether real learning has taken place. Following are step-by-step instructions for implementing this type of pre-/post-test within the context of upper-level discipline-based instruction:

Step 1: Develop learning outcomes (what students should be able to do) relevant to a class assignment in a subject-based discipline. (For example, faculty might want students to be able to search for and identify primary research articles in order to write a systematic review of evidence-based nursing research.)

Step 2: Design an authentic pre-/post-test assessment instrument based on the class learning outcome. (For example, this instrument might include questions that ask students to perform specific tasks relevant to finding primary research articles and then reflect on their performance.)

Step 3: Email pre-test to faculty for posting in the learning management system or deliver hard copies for distribution during class. Faculty then assign the pre-test as a take-home assignment, ideally at the end of the first class session.

Step 4: Collect completed pre-tests from faculty member. Assess pre-tests for students' ability to answer questions and/or perform specific tasks as well as for the content of their reflections.

Step 5: Design instruction session to address gaps in student knowledge or common misunderstandings.

Step 6: At the end of the face-to-face instruction session, distribute post-test and have students complete it and hand it in.

Step 7: Assess post-tests in comparison to pre-tests. Share results with faculty and revise lesson plans if necessary, particularly if students continue to struggle with important concepts.

Writing/Research Assignments and Presentations

Assessing information literacy proficiencies with writing or research assignments and presentations can pose the same difficulties as annotated bibliographies in that it can be difficult to tease out the impact of library instruction on the final product, particularly if students received only one instruction session or completed a set of asynchronous online tutorials. This problem is especially acute when library instruction occurs toward the beginning of the semester and the writing assignment is completed toward the end of the semester. However, there are situations in which presentations can provide an authentic summative information literacy assessment, especially if the library instruction session is designed to support student presentations and if the assignment includes elements specific to that instruction. In addition, if student presentations occur within approximately one to two weeks after instruction, then it may be possible to measure the impact of library instruction on those presentations. In this case, as with other summative assessments, faculty-librarian collaboration is key to developing learning outcomes and for obtaining

Sample 6.9. Pre-/Post-Test Questions

1. You are conducting a systematic review of the nursing literature on the effect of exercise as a health intervention for children with diabetes. Where would you begin to search for primary research articles on this topic?

2. What search terms would you use to find articles on this topic in the resource you listed above?

3. Write the citation information for one primary research article you found on this topic using the resource and search terms you listed above.

4. How can you tell that the article you cited is primary rather than secondary research?

5. Did you revise your search terms in order to find the article you cited? Why or why not?

6. Was it difficult to find a primary research article on this topic? Why or why not?

access to the assessment instrument, which in this case would involve attending the student presentations. For example, a faculty member might assign a five-minute oral presentation on a specific topic, such as a contemporary social issue. In order to complete the assignment, students might need to find a recent article, study, commentary, or news report on the topic and closely analyze its content. During the presentation, students might be asked to discuss how their source presents the issue and then provide a commentary on it, part of which would involve evaluating the quality and/or validity of the source. In this case the librarian would design an instruction session that focuses on finding and evaluating the source material for these presentations. During the presentations, the librarian assesses each student's ability to find and evaluate their source material, while the faculty member assesses the student's analytical skills and ability to present. If the librarian implements a formative assessment instrument during the instruction session, such as an authentic minute paper or a performative task-based worksheet, those artifacts could then be compared with the results of the student presentations to develop a better understanding of students' ability to transfer their knowledge from the hands-on practice of the instruction session to the preparation and delivery of their presentations, providing librarians with more meaningful information about student learning. The results of these assessments could then be shared with the faculty member and other stakeholders in order to demonstrate the importance of information literacy instruction for student learning and academic performance.

Search Logs

Search logs are another form of summative assessment that can be readily implemented in the most common instructional settings and, when combined with a formative assessment such as a task-based worksheet, can provide librarians with an authentic measure of student learning. Though search logs are more easily assigned within credit-bearing information literacy classes, embedded librarianship, and other long-form instruction, they can also be employed in asynchronous online instruction and one-shot sessions. For example, if a search log is included as part of a performative task-based worksheet in a one-shot session, it provides the teaching librarian with one exercise/assessment instrument that gathers both formative and summative authentic assessment data. In this case, after the students complete the assigned task or set of tasks, they are prompted to document their search strategies and the resources they used to complete the search, and then reflect on their choices. In addition, this type of exercise might also prompt students to compare how their search strategies worked in different environments, such as two different databases or a library database and Google Scholar, and then discuss why they might use one or the other to complete an assignment. The advantage of this type of assessment within a one-shot session is that it serves as both a formative assessment of a task-based activity and a summative assessment that can help to document knowledge transfer and higher-order thinking. In addition, this type of assessment can be easily adapted from a more typical task-based worksheet—especially a worksheet that includes a reflection component—by replacing the reflection prompts with a search log exercise to be completed after the assigned tasks. Thus, the process for implementing a combined task-based/search log assignment would be quite similar to the methods outlined in the section in this chapter on performative task-based assignments, with only the last portion of the worksheet revised to include the search log prompts. Moreover, performative task-based assignments that include search logs act as authentic teaching and learning tools that provide librarians with both formative and summative assessment data that can be leveraged internally to improve teaching effectiveness and externally to demonstrate the library's commitment to student learning. Following are step-by-step instructions for implementing this type of task-based search log assignment into a single instruction session in any setting:

Step 1: Develop learning outcomes (what students should be able to do) relevant to the class assignment and design a worksheet that asks students to perform tasks related to that learning outcome. (For example, faculty might require that students use at least one scholarly source for their papers. In this case, you would design a task that allows the students to come away with that source as well as the ability to find additional scholarly sources on their own.) This worksheet should require students to complete a set of tasks, document their search process, and explain why they took each step.

Step 2: Design an instruction session that scaffolds students through increasingly complex tasks, using each task to build on and reinforce the prior task.

Step 3: Allot most of the session time to hands-on practice and discussion, roaming as students complete each task and using questions and obstacles to provide immediate feedback as well as librarian- and peer-teaching moments.

Step 4: Have students hand in the worksheets when completed. If time allows, close the loop by initiating a discussion about how students completed the task.

Step 5: Assess the performative task-based worksheets for the students' ability to complete the tasks, as well as their ability to revise and refine their search strategies.

Step 6: Email students with additional feedback to correct their mistakes or misperceptions or to answer any lingering questions.

Step 7: Revise instruction based on common tasks or concepts with which students continue to struggle.

Finally, it should be apparent that there are a substantial number of formative and summative authentic assessment techniques that can be readily adapted to most instructional settings. In addition, while many of the sample exercises presented in this chapter are designed as paper-based worksheets (for reasons outlined earlier), they can be delivered in a number of other formats, including shared Google documents, free polling software, and as many others as a librarian's creativity allows. With authentic assessment, the delivery method is less important than an instrument's

---

Sample 6.10. Search Log Prompts

Tell us about the process you used to find a scholarly journal article on your topic.

In what database or other resource did you start your search? After you began searching, did you switch to a different resource? Why or why not?

List the keywords you used to begin your search. Did you have to revise your search? Why or why not?

List the keywords you used to find the article listed above.

Did you find it difficult to develop search terms that provided you with good results? Why or why not?

How would you advise another student to begin searching for scholarly articles? Please be specific.

---

ability to foster deeper student learning and provide librarians with rich information about their teaching effectiveness. A well-designed authentic assessment offers not only rich internal data on both but also the kind of information that can be shared with external stakeholders to demonstrate the library's commitment to institutional teaching and learning goals. Now that we have had a look at the current state of authentic assessment for information literacy instruction, including how to adapt its techniques to a number of different settings, the next chapter will offer a look at future directions in authentic teaching, learning, and assessment.

REFERENCES

Bell, Steven. 2008. "Keeping Them Enrolled: How Academic Libraries Contribute to Student Retention." *Library Issues* 29, no. 1 (September): 1–4.

Head, Alison J. 2013. "Learning the Ropes: How Freshmen Conduct Course Research Once They Enter College." *Project Information Literacy*. December 5. http://www.projectinfolit. org/uploads/2/7/5/4/27541717/pil_2013_freshmenstudy_fullreportv2.pdf.

Mueller, P.A., and D.M. Oppenheimer. 2014. "The Pen Is Mightier Than the Keyboard: Advantages of Longhand over Laptop Note Taking." *Psychological Science* 25, no. 6 (June): 1159–68.

Sherriff, Graham. 2017. "Guide on the Side and LibWizard Tutorials Side-By-Side: How Do the Two Platforms for Split-Screen Online Tutorials Compare?" *Journal of Web Librarianship* 11, no. 2 (April–June): 124–42.

Thomas, Susan, Eamon Tewell, and Gloria Willson. 2017. "Where Students Start and What They Do When They Get Stuck: A Qualitative Inquiry into Academic Information-Seeking and Help-Seeking Practices." *Journal of Academic Librarianship* 43, no. 3 (May): 224–31.

University of Arizona Libraries. 2017. "About Guide on the Side." code.library, October 4. http://code.library.arizona.edu.

7

Future Directions in Authentic Assessment

While authentic assessment for information literacy instruction is still a fairly new concept, the seeds of its future can be discerned in the literature on authentic assessment across educational contexts. From the assessment of the need for early intervention in toddlers to the increasingly complex assessment data reported out to higher education funding agencies and other important stakeholders, the need for authentic, as opposed to standardized, assessment will only increase in importance as a means to understand what students—at any stage of their lives—can actually do in the long term rather than simply what they can commit to short-term memory or even perform within a controlled context. For example, researchers in early childhood education have determined that, among other factors, "the changing demographics of the population" have created a mismatch between traditional standardized evaluations, which demonstrate "the increased need to explore and use the most evidence-based and authentic assessment tools available with infants and toddlers to minimize the discrepancy between the needs of the child and the manner in which the needs are determined through evaluation" (de Sam Lazaro 2017). This mismatch can also be detected in colleges and universities where the student population is not only more diverse but is increasingly composed of international students who have entirely divergent backgrounds and widely different expectations for their educational experience. Authentic assessment can help provide the kind of evidence demonstrating that students are both learning and are able to apply that learning to solve problems both in the school setting and in the workplace. Therefore, this chapter will examine the current trends for authentic and evidence-based assessment across institutional contexts as well as discuss their implications for librarians going forward.

In higher education, authentic and other assessment techniques vary widely based on academic discipline. For instance, writing-intensive courses in many humanities-based disciplines have often employed authentic teaching and assessment methodologies, such as the flipped classroom and performative task-based assignments, that have only recently been adapted to STEM subjects or to the business classroom. If the goal of authentic assessment is to seamlessly incorporate teaching, learning, and assessment into one organic whole, the humanities have been focused on this method for many years. For example, faculty teaching English literature require their students to read and synthesize material outside of class and then come to class prepared to discuss it, which is the model of a flipped classroom. In addition, students in these classes are assessed based on whether they can accomplish a set of tasks, such as writing a critical analysis of a particular text or creating an annotated bibliography, and are often required to revise their work based on feedback from their instructor. However, outside this context many academic disciplines, including library instruction, have relied on fixed-answer quizzes, multiple-choice exams, and other modes of assessment that are relatively easy to administer but provide very little real information about long-term student learning. Without requiring students to demonstrate their learning so that they might integrate new knowledge into their established mental frameworks, very few claims can be made about whether students actually learned anything at all as opposed to memorizing a set of facts that they either do or do not retain over time. And even if students retain some, or even all, of those facts over time, what good are the facts unless students can synthesize and apply them to create new knowledge? While the STEM subjects most often rely on more standardized testing techniques, it is especially important for students studying these subjects to be able to contextualize, to create a whole out of the accumulated facts that they memorize. For example, in the health sciences, facts without context can prevent practitioners from making a correct diagnosis—in the old adage, they might miss the forest for the trees. Authentic assessment can help educators understand what students are truly learning, measure what they can do, and address the gaps in their knowledge. Thus, authentic assessment is gaining ground in higher education across disciplines that have traditionally used standardized testing to measure student performance, including subjects such as English as a Foreign Language (EFL) and English as a Second Language (ESL). Researchers in this field are now advocating for changing traditional assessment techniques to methods that "tell us if students can apply what they have learned in authentic situations," noting that "if a student does well on a test of knowledge we might infer that the student could also apply that knowledge. But, we could more directly check for the ability to apply by asking the student to use what they have learned in some meaningful way" (Ortega and Minchala 2017).

This distinction between tests of knowledge and the ability to apply that knowledge is at the heart of authentic assessment and can be especially difficult to implement within K–12 education, with its emphasis on standardized testing, particularly in the STEM disciplines. That said, there are many secondary school educators around the world grappling with this issue in creative ways. For example, teachers in North Carolina worked with four secondary schools to create performance-based assessments for STEM subjects, piloting the initial design with classes in earth and environmental science. In this case, engineering and science educators created a "performance task process" that "required students to move through four types of activities: research, brainstorming, exploration, and reflection" (Potter, Ernst, and Glennie 2017). In other words, this process included all the key components of authentic assessment and encouraged students to engage in higher-order thinking to successfully complete the tasks. Most interestingly, at the end of the pilot project, the implementation of performance-based assessment resulted in "student performance proficiency in excess of 60%," with the majority of students scoring proficient in science and mathematics on their standardized exams. Moreover, as the "performance tasks became more complex, the proficiency rate increased," which reinforces the idea that the integration of authentic teaching and learning strategies, including authentic assessment, not only encourages higher-order thinking but also results in "higher-level cognitive abilities and multiple-subject proficiency."

This type of assessment in secondary education, also known internationally as "assessment for learning (AfL)," has often been considered less rigorous or professional than standardized testing that uses formal statistical techniques to measure student achievement. However, because "interaction between the assessor and the learner is key to it" and these "assessments are often teacher-designed and may be part of the classroom dialogue," it can be argued that it is only through this type of assessment that "students' understanding can be gauged well" (Baird et al. 2017). Thus the case is continuing to be made that an assessment instrument that does not actually measure students' understanding of a subject but instead focuses on easily quantifiable numerical measures tells us very little about student learning. As a result, researchers focusing on assessment in secondary education have begun to increasingly advocate for a new understanding of learning theory that takes "into account the dynamic relationships between curriculum exposure, assessment design and learning outcomes," which tracks closely to the authentic teaching, learning, and assessment techniques discussed earlier. Interestingly, considering the volume of testing at the secondary level that takes place around the world, some researchers still find it "puzzling that we have not gained more from those data regarding student learning" (Baird et al. 2017), worrying that teacher-designed AfL instruments cannot be properly systematized. However, this focus on quantitative measures as opposed to performance-based appraisals tends to privilege data over learning and measurement over understanding. While large datasets derived from standardized testing are undeniably attractive in that they allow us to compare student achievement longitudinally, independent of the context in which those students live or study, they do not do a particularly good job of explaining whether students understood what they learned well enough to apply it across educational or professional contexts. If a student learns how to write well, as demonstrated by a variety of written artifacts, it might be understood that the student would be able to transfer that skill to another class or into the workplace.

But if a student demonstrated that he or she had memorized a chemical formula well enough to answer a question correctly on a standardized test, does that mean that the student will be able to take that knowledge and apply it in the lab? This question is key to understanding the difference between authentic assessment and other forms of testing. Authentic assessment attempts to measure whether students have learned material well enough to apply it outside of the classroom and over time.

Indeed, while it is ever more understood that the current challenge, particularly in the developed world, is to teach students how "to solve problems and to reason, to exercise personal judgement and go beyond the routine," assessment in the United States, in particular, "continues to focus largely on how many 'bits and pieces' of information students have accumulated and how quickly they can access them" (Resnick and Schantz 2017), which is increasingly out of step with the psychology of learning and cognition. Moreover, the complex world into which students graduate requires them to synthesize and analyze a wide array of information sources to make informed judgments in both their personal and working lives. Thus, an educational environment in which students learn "bits and pieces" but are not assessed on whether they can put those bits and pieces together (synthesize), understand their meaning as a whole (analyze), and then use that meaning to solve problems (apply) fails both teachers and students and "actually works against the educational imperatives of our time." Interestingly, as noted earlier, authentic teaching, learning, and assessment is not necessarily a new concept and has been practiced across humanities disciplines since those disciplines were first taught. Moreover, integrating teaching and assessment and requiring students to produce performance-based artifacts has long been considered part of the "daily practice of learning," but only in a limited number of disciplines. The current challenge includes reproducing this type of authentic teaching, learning, and assessment across every subject, as well as convincing stakeholders that this type of assessment, while not as easy to measure, is not only fair but also matches "our learning goals for students," helps build their minds, and enables "them to create the new knowledge our societies need." Many researchers believe that it is imperative that educational institutions at every level—from preschool through college—begin to address the mismatch between how and what is being taught and the needs of the twenty-first-century learner.

Given the increasing academic emphasis on the STEM disciplines, authentic teaching and learning at every level within that context is becoming increasingly prevalent "especially within STEM academy, magnet, and strand school formats" (Ernst, Glennie, and Li 2017). As noted earlier, many secondary STEM classrooms are beginning to grapple with performance- and task-based assessment. Indeed, "the recently released Next Generation Science Standards (NGSS) emphasize eight 'practices' in K–12 science" and, most interestingly, "students' performance is considered as an indispensable way to demonstrate competency on knowledge and skills specific to each practice in science learning." However, implementation of these new methods can be spotty and result in "proficiency separations" between schools, even when the same authentic teaching, learning, and assessment strategies are employed. These performance variations might be attributed to teachers' "attitudes and willingness of implementation as well as their strategies in scaffolding and supporting students." Moreover, prior research on this topic indicates that "teachers might consider that problem-based assessments" are "time-consuming and difficult to implement." This last point is especially relevant for teaching librarians, since they often have very little time in which to teach and assess information literacy competencies. If teachers in secondary schools who work with their students for a significant amount of time every week feel that problem-based learning and assessment is too difficult and time-consuming to employ, this challenge is especially acute for librarians across most instructional contexts, including embedded librarians, since their time with students is so limited.

Nonetheless, because the types of tasks and assessments that measure "student procedural knowledge and higher-order thinking abilities" (Ernst, Glennie, and Li 2017) are crucial to understanding whether students can apply their knowledge, techniques that promote that type of learning and assessment are also becoming increasingly important for STEM education in colleges and universities. While "the number of students who start and do not complete" degrees in STEM disciplines "ranges from 40 to 60 percent" (Stieha, Shadle, and Paterson 2016), employment in STEM-related jobs grew by 10.5 percent from May 2009 to May 2015, more than double the growth in non-STEM jobs (Fayer, Lacey, and Watson 2017), which indicates a mismatch between the needs of twenty-first-century employers and the number of graduates in those fields. Therefore, improving teaching and learning in STEM disciplines is more urgently needed than ever to retain undergraduates in those subjects and encourage them to complete their degrees. In addition, since the American Association of Colleges and Universities considers educating "scientifically literate citizens" to be an "essential component of a liberal education" (Stieha, Shadle, and Paterson 2016), authentic teaching, learning, and assessment strategies, whether for STEM majors or within general education STEM classes, can help fulfill that charge. However, faculty continue to encounter "disconnections between teaching practice and learning outcomes assessment," which echoes the experience of teaching librarians. Many instructors, whether teachers in K12 schools, faculty in higher education institutions, or instruction librarians, find it difficult to implement authentic assessment because of that disconnect. In other words, it can be a challenge to reframe assessment as an integral part of teaching rather than as separate from it. As we have seen, authentic assessment presupposes changing the way teachers teach in order to improve student learning. It also asks instructors to rethink both student learning outcomes and the methodology for measuring those outcomes. This dual charge can pose a real challenge, especially for teachers in subjects, such as STEM and information literacy, where this type of instruction imposes a dramatic change on prior practice and upends settled understandings. However, as difficult as changing teaching and assessment practices can be, to improve student learning outcomes as well as student persistence, courses need to be redesigned "to include evidence-based instructional practices and authentic assessment" (Stieha, Shadle, and Paterson 2016).

Since information literacy is a key component of scientific literacy, and indeed of many other discipline-specific literacies, it is imperative that teaching librarians also rethink their pedagogical practice. As we have seen in prior chapters, authentic teaching, learning, and assessment are accessible to librarians across almost every instructional setting. In addition, information literacy instruction, especially in the first year, is foundational to students' success as they progress through their education. If a student fails to understand an important basic concept, such as how to distinguish a reliable source from an unreliable one, then advanced subject-specific literacies become more difficult to achieve. Without a strong base of knowledge, especially in an increasingly complex information environment, students will struggle to find, evaluate, and incorporate sources into their knowledge bases in order not only to successfully complete their assignments but also to create new knowledge, which is at the heart of the academic enterprise. Therefore, improving teaching and learning is just as important in the library as it is in the discipline-specific classroom. Authentic assessment is central to developing a greater understanding of what students learn and whether they can apply it. For example, librarians at Metropolitan State University of Denver redesigned their instructional practices in order both to teach and measure student learning in a more authentic way, recognizing the importance of focusing on concepts such as evaluation rather than traditional Boolean searching and database selection because the "curriculum requires students to find, analyze, and integrate arguments from different types of information sources, including popular and scholarly articles" (Fisher and Seeber 2017). If librarians do not engage with the basic contours of the current information landscape and teach students how to navigate information sources—no matter where they find them—library instructors will do students a great disservice, not only in terms of their educational success but also in terms of their civic participation as informed citizens. This type of instructional approach, along with authentic assessment techniques that attempt to measure actual student learning, is more critical than ever. Nonetheless, many librarians continue to be uncomfortable with this method, worrying that more "discussion-based, not demonstration-based" sessions are difficult to lead. In addition, they express concerns about the marginalization of library databases, as well as their discomfort with facilitating large-group discussions (Fisher and Seeber 2017). Some of these concerns can be addressed by providing better support for teaching librarians, including ongoing workshops within academic libraries, continuing education programs, and perhaps mandatory classes on pedagogy in graduate schools of library and information science. However, despite residual librarian discomfort, and as the development of the ACRL Framework indicates, library lesson plans and assessments that focus on teaching broad concepts rather than discrete skills and that encourage "deep and critical thinking" point the way forward for information literacy. This type of approach demonstrates not only the continued relevance but truly the continued centrality of libraries and librarians to student success.

Along with completing their education, external stakeholders such as accrediting bodies and the federal government also measure student success by how well students are prepared to enter the workplace and to remain employable. Since "the fluid workplace requires employees to be more professionally nimble" than ever before, the twenty-first-century workforce is required to stay informed in a more dramatic way and in an environment in which "pathways to, and the uses of, information have become far more complex" (Head 2017). Moreover, "a study by the National Association of Colleges and Employers (NACE) . . . closely aligns with the value of information literacy competencies at hiring time." These competencies include the recruits' "ability to obtain and process information for planning and making decisions." As we have seen, performative task-based assessment and problem-based activities both address this type of need, encouraging students to use and evaluate information to complete specific tasks or solve real-life information problems. However, Project Information Literacy's workplace study found "a wide discrepancy between the information competencies employers say they need, and the skills that recent university graduates demonstrated in the workplace once they were hired." Instead of employees who could find the "quickest answers to an information problem," they needed to "hire patient and persistent researchers" (Head 2017). This patience and persistence can be a difficult habit to cultivate with students, who are accustomed to using their smartphones to answer their questions and tend to rely on the first few results that pop up in their search engines. Librarians who teach information literacy often emphasize that research is an iterative process, that search strategies require ongoing revision, and that it takes patience to do it well. This type of persistence is the kind of "transferable information skill" that will help students "succeed in the workplace and as lifelong learners when they graduate." An iterative research process is encouraged when students are asked to engage with it directly during library instruction. Moreover, many of the techniques for authentic teaching, learning, and assessment during library instruction sessions described in previous chapters require students to think more deeply about the research process and explain what worked for them, what didn't work, and why. That engagement encourages higher-order thinking and generates an awareness of the process of research rather than just the result. As noted earlier, there are many ways in which to engage students in the library classroom, and "the challenge for librarians now, and into the near future, will be developing teaching methods that help to create a culture of persistent question asking and to help students develop the skills—both traditional and high tech—to continue learning on their own" (Head 2017). Authentic teaching strategies encourage the persistent question asking so important for developing the kinds of skills necessary for today's students, whether in the classroom or in the workplace, and authentic assessment helps us more clearly determine whether students are developing those important skills.

As Fisher and Seeber mention, after developing and implementing authentic teaching, learning, and assessment of information literacy in a programmatic way, librarians also need to gather substantial data on its results (Fisher and Seeber 2017). In addition, it is crucial that this data be comparable from one session to the next, both for reporting out and for instructional improvement. If teaching librarians use the same lesson plan and assessment instrument for each section of a first-year instruction program, for example, those assessments can be compared from section to section and provide substantial evidence of the library's centrality to the institutional teaching and learning mission. Moreover, consistent lesson plans and assessments can be used to support teaching librarians who might need help developing their pedagogy and engaging students in the classroom. This kind of consistency can help librarians communicate a level of seriousness about education for information literacy that has often appeared to be lacking—at least from perspectives outside of the library—and help solve some of the difficulties many librarians express with getting faculty and administrative buy-in for instruction programs. To be taken seriously as colleagues within the academy, librarians equally need to demonstrate a level of seriousness about their work in it. In addition, as authentic assessment practices become increasingly common in higher education, there is an opportunity for librarians to develop expertise in this important institutional priority, which is a result of "increased attention from accreditors, the federal and state governments, and the public" (Sullivan and McConnell 2017). Campuses "of all types and sizes" are developing more authentic and "learner-centered assessment strategies," which are being driven by "concerns over the use of one-size-fits-all approaches, such as standardized tests." And if "faculty practices must change if college student learning of both disciplinary content and higher-order skills is to meet 21st Century needs and expectations" (Sullivan and McConnell 2017), then the practices of teaching librarians must also change. Given the well-documented challenges to faculty-librarian collaboration, demonstrating expertise in achieving a significant institutional outcome offers an opportunity for librarians to help lead the conversation rather than simply react to stakeholder needs.

As we approach the end of the second decade of the twenty-first century, the future direction of effective teaching, learning, and assessment across institutional contexts and into the workplace is starting to become clear. The convergence of a complex information environment along with pressure from internal and external institutional stakeholders requires all teachers—from preschool through graduate school—to rethink learning outcomes, the methods for achieving those outcomes, and the techniques for measuring them. While the early part of this century saw the increased implementation of standardized testing in secondary schools, it has since become apparent that these tests, while providing robust data and statistics, need to be, at the very least, supplemented with more evidence-based assessments that are better able to measure authentic student learning. Academic librarians need to recognize and embrace the challenges and opportunities inherent in this changing environment, since the library will no more be exempt from these pressures than any other part of the academy. While assessment in libraries attempts to measure their impact on the larger institution, often using such quantitative measures as the number of books checked out or the number of students who walk through the doors, or attempting to correlate the frequency of library use with student success, authentic teaching and learning strategies have the potential to demonstrate value in a way that is core to an institution's educational mission. It has long been a goal of academic librarians to transform the thinking about libraries within higher education, moving them from being considered a somewhat peripheral support service to being thought of as central to the teaching and learning enterprise. This type of transformation requires that librarians engage with disciplines outside of library science and revise their teaching and assessment to incorporate both theory and practice from other areas. Database demonstrations alone are no longer adequate for conveying crucial information literacy concepts. Indeed, the term *information literacy* itself implies a greater understanding of the structure of information and how and why that structure exists than can be conveyed to students using more traditional library instruction methods. An increasingly complex information environment requires librarians to address it in new and more effective ways. Moreover, assessing students' ability to synthesize, analyze, and apply their skills in navigating this complicated landscape also needs to change. In this case, fixed-answer quizzes are just as inadequate as database demonstrations for teaching and assessing the twenty-first-century student. Instead, authentic teaching, learning, and assessment have the potential to address the urgent imperatives of improved student learning, expanded stakeholder requirements, and changing workplace needs. Going forward, just as new positions are being created for data and digital scholarship librarians that address the evolution of the twenty-first-century library, so too will information literacy librarians be tasked with rethinking how and what we teach and measuring how and what students learn. Engaging with authentic assessment can enable instruction librarians to demonstrate the foundational importance of library instruction to developing concomitant literacies such as scientific, quantitative, media, and technological literacy. Finally, the next chapter will sum up where these techniques have been, where they are now, and what librarians can do with them.

REFERENCES

Baird, Jo-Anne, David Andrich, Therese N. Hopfenbeck, and Gordon Stobart. 2017. "Assessment and Learning: Fields Apart?" *Assessment in Education: Principles, Policy and Practice* 24, no. 3 (August): 317–50.

de Sam Lazaro, Stephanie Lynn. 2017. "The Importance of Authentic Assessments in Eligibility Determination for Infants and Toddlers." *Journal of Early Intervention* 39, no. 2 (June): 88–105.

Ernst, Jeremy V., Elizabeth Glennie, and Songze Li. 2017. "Performance-Based Task Assessment of Higher-Order Proficiencies in Redesigned STEM High Schools." *Contemporary Issues in Education Research* 10, no. 1 (First Quarter): 13–32.

Fayer, Stella, Alan Lacey, and Audrey Watson. 2017. "STEM Occupations: Past, Present, and Future." *U.S. Bureau of Labor Statistics Spotlight on Statistics*, January 1. https://www.bls.gov/spotlight/2017/science-technology-engineering-and-mathematics-stem-occupations-past-present-and-future/pdf/science-technology-engineering-and-mathematics-stem-occupations-past-present-and-future.pdf.

Fisher, Zoe, and Kevin Seeber. 2017. "Finding Foundations: A Model for Information Literacy Assessment of First-Year Students." *In the Library with the Lead Pipe* (August): 1.

Head, Alison J. 2017. "Posing the Million-Dollar Question: What Happens after Graduation?" *Journal of Information Literacy* 11, no. 1 (June): 80–90.

Ortega, Diego P., and Olga E. Minchala. 2017. "Assessing Students in an Authentic and Ongoing Manner in the English Classroom." *Theory and Practice in Language Studies* 7, no. 3 (March): 159–65.

Potter, Barry S., Jeremy V. Ernst, and Elizabeth J. Glennie. 2017. "Performance-Based Assessment in the Secondary STEM Classroom." *Technology and Engineering Teacher* 76, no. 6 (March): 18–22.

Resnick, Lauren B., and Faith Schantz. 2017. "Testing, Teaching, Learning: Who Is in Charge?" *Assessment in Education: Principles, Policy and Practice* 24, no. 3 (August): 424–32.

Stieha, Vicki, Susan E. Shadle, and Sharon Paterson. 2016. "Stirring the Pot: Supporting and Challenging General Education Science, Technology, Engineering, and Mathematics Faculty to Change Teaching and Assessment Practice." *Journal of General Education* 65, no. 2 (April): 85–109.

Sullivan, Daniel F., and Kate Drezek McConnell. 2017. "Big Progress in Authentic Assessment, but by Itself Not Enough." *Change: The Magazine of Higher Learning* 49, no. 1 (March): 14–25.

8

Authentic Assessment, the ACRL Framework, and Beyond

Authentic assessment in primary, secondary, and higher education, in the discipline-specific and library classroom, has been discussed, debated, implemented, and argued for many years. Educators continue to grapple with questions such as: Why do we have to "assess?" What does it mean to assess? What are we trying to assess? Can we compare assessments from one year to the next? What does assessment tell us about teaching and learning? These, and other, questions are important to ask as a prelude to beginning any type of assessment program. As we have seen, authentic assessment is inseparable from teaching and learning. To assess student learning, librarians need to integrate teaching and assessment into one seamless whole, integrating teaching practice with measuring student learning. Moreover, while understanding and implementing these methods can be a challenge, it is a challenge worth undertaking in an academic environment in which student needs seem to have outstripped both traditional methods of teaching and modes of assessment. Nevertheless, the chapters in this volume should enable librarians to recognize and work with authentic assessment in any instructional context—from one-shot sessions to credit-bearing courses, from face-to-face to asynchronous online tutorials—demonstrating their commitment to excellent teaching, enhanced student learning, and the goals of both institutional and outside stakeholders.

As we have seen, the conversation around authentic assessment of information literacy instruction has been growing for the past ten years, with reported implementations and case studies steadily increasing. Given the need not only to assess the library's impact on the student experience but also to demonstrate the library's centrality to the academic teaching and learning mission, authentic assessment can provide compelling evidence of the instruction librarian's role in supporting student success. Because there is such a wide range of formative and summative assessments available to teaching librarians, adapting authentic assessment to the library classroom has taken an equally large number of forms. For example, credit-bearing classes, embedded librarians, and faculty-librarian collaborations have all employed annotated bibliographies as authentic summative assessments. In addition, librarians teaching one-shot sessions have used authentic formative assessments such as minute papers, performative task-based assignments, and problem-based activities to provide evidence of both student learning and teaching effectiveness. Given their flexibility and adaptability, performative task-based assignments, whether designed as a paper-based worksheet that is completed during the instruction session or embedded into asynchronous online tutorials, are currently the most commonly used authentic assessments across instructional contexts. Because these assignments require students to synthesize, analyze, and apply their learning to completing a specific task, they can be used as either a formative or summative assessment, depending on the needs of the class. These types of assignments can be designed as authentic task-based minute papers completed at the end of one class in a credit-bearing course or can be woven into a one-shot session as both a teaching and learning tool as well as a measure of that teaching and learning. In any case, authentic formative and summative assessment instruments tell a more complete story about student learning—and librarian teaching—than fixed-answer quizzes and satisfaction surveys.

Nevertheless, the advantages of authentic teaching, learning, and assessment also contain their concomitant challenges. This type of evidence-based practice requires librarians to rethink what we teach, how we teach it, and what we measure. Switching from skills-based instruction to concept-based instruction can be a difficult transition to make, especially if a librarian has been teaching a class for a long time and feels comfortable with a specific method. Moreover, this challenge is not limited to teaching librarians. As we have seen, teachers at all levels continue to struggle with these concepts, many observing that authentic assessment can be time consuming, difficult to implement, and not as easily quantifiable as traditional fixed-answer quizzes and tests. However, as demonstrated in previous chapters, the advantages of this method far outweigh its challenges since it can provide teachers with a far more accurate picture of the student learning that is, or perhaps is not, taking place. In addition, at its best authentic teaching, learning, and assessment encourage higher-order thinking and knowledge transfer, promoting habits of mind that empower students to engage more deeply and think more critically about their own learning practice. Asking students to answer the "why" questions about their own learning is just as important as answering students' "why" questions during class. The reflective nature of authentic methods encourages both teacher and student to consider not only what they are learning but how they are learning it and how they might use what they have learned across contexts. Reflection encourages students to apply what they have learned and use it to solve problems and create new knowledge.

Librarians can also benefit from this type of reflection and begin to ask questions about what we want students to learn—and then work backward to how we teach them what they need to know and how we measure whether they are learning what we think they are. The ACRL Framework for Information Literacy for Higher Education (ACRL 2015) is a good place to start this type of reflection. For example, the Framework outlines six very broad information literacy learning outcomes but does not necessarily explain when and in what order these concepts should be taught or what methods should be used to teach them, presenting librarians with a flexible set of guidelines that can at first seem daunting to implement. However, even though designing instruction around the Framework can seem difficult, its very flexibility also liberates teaching librarians from the far more proscriptive and skills-based standards that preceded it. Moreover, the Framework is eminently adaptable to authentic teaching and learning, since it encourages the teaching of broad-based concepts such as evaluation ("Authority Is Constructed and Contextual"), revision ("Searching as Strategic Exploration"), and the construction of effective keyword searches ("Research as Inquiry"), all of which map to the old standards but also allow librarians to engage in the type of metacognitive thinking that authentic assessment presumes. In addition, many of the case studies examined in earlier chapters emphasize the effectiveness of teaching a few broad-based concepts and focusing on higher-order information literacy rather than simple database searching skills. In other words, conceptual understanding needs to take precedence over mechanical proficiency. For too many years, library instruction has often seemed to proceed from the premise that teaching students how to construct a keyword search and then find articles in a database would provide them with the skills they need to succeed at college-level research. But it has become increasingly apparent that while students might be able to find an article in a database, they have no idea how to evaluate that article for its credibility or use it to construct an argument. And while it can be argued that it is not the librarian's job to teach students how to construct an argument, it *is* a librarian's job to teach students how to evaluate information so that they can differentiate between information types and choose the appropriate type of information to accomplish a specific purpose. This skill has become especially important as students experience overwhelming information overload and continue to rely on the research strategies they used in high school. If librarians, especially those who teach first-year students, fail to address these issues, the students will fail to master the basic competencies of information literacy.

Authentic teaching, learning, and assessment can help librarians address the ACRL Framework in library instruction, as well as measure both student learning and their teaching effectiveness. For example, chapter 6 outlines how to adapt this methodology to the most common instructional setting, including how to design both the instruction session and the assessment instrument. In addition, the section in that chapter on performative task-based assignments outlines a sample lesson plan for a one-shot instruction session using a scaffolded method that addresses students' prior knowledge. This type of lesson can also be implemented in a way that addresses all six of the frames outlined by the ACRL. For example, in activating students' prior knowledge of searching Google and Wikipedia, instruction librarians can use it as a point to introduce the frame that "information has value," discussing not only whether an article is open access or freely available, but also that their personal information has value—especially for advertisers and marketers. This discussion can also introduce the idea that "authority is constructed and contextual" by teaching students how to differentiate between the types of information found on the web (including analyzing domains, pointing out authorship, and much more) and contrasting it with the type of information students might find in a journal database or a reputable reference resource, including answering the "why" questions about what they find where and how it gets to them. This discussion can lead directly into a conversation about information types and where they fit into the information ecosystem, introducing the idea of "scholarship as conversation." Once students' prior knowledge has been activated and new information has found a place within their mental framework, students can then be taught how to use background information from reliable sources to develop search terms that they can use to find more scholarly information, which addresses the idea of "research as inquiry." At each point during the lesson, the librarian can encourage students to practice searching and evaluating and share and compare their results, completing tasks such as mapping out alternate terms and key concepts, creating keyword searches, finding background information, adding new terms to their search, and expanding and narrowing their topics. After students have practiced some of the basics and developed a keyword search, the librarian can then demonstrate searching in a library database or discovery layer using a keyword search mapped out collectively during the lesson, showing students how to revise their searches based on the results they find—which introduces them to "searching as strategic exploration." Finally, as students begin to find and evaluate scholarly journal articles, librarians can introduce them to the idea of "information creation as process," not just the scholarly process that has been outlined during class but also their own process in creating new knowledge from the information that they find, using analogies to compare what they are being asked to do as students to the scholarly process itself. At each point during this lesson, students are being asked to synthesize new information, analyze it, and apply it to completing specific tasks. At the end of the lesson, students complete a written reflection that asks them to think about their own thinking, answering prompts that help them frame what they have learned to aid them in transferring their skills outside the library classroom—both during their time as students and afterward as informed citizens. In this case, the teaching librarian not only addresses all six of the frames but also employs authentic teaching and assessment—all within a one-shot session.

Therefore, rather than thinking of the ACRL Framework and assessment as separate components, it might be more valuable to think of them as inextricably entwined, offering teaching librarians a broad-based and flexible set of learning outcomes that can be adapted to each institution and instructional context, providing a starting point for designing lesson plans and assessment instruments that more authentically measure student learning and more realistically address the twenty-first-century information landscape. For example, the ACRL's "Information Literacy Competency Standards for Higher Education" (ACRL 2000), while emphasizing the "uncertain quality and expanding quantity of information" and recognizing that this situation poses "large challenges for society," still provided a more concrete skills-based set of competencies and learning outcomes that allowed librarians to focus instruction on lower-order skills such as identifying keywords and synonyms and searching a database to "access the needed information effectively and efficiently." While the competency standards also emphasized the extent to which higher-order skills are necessary and should be assessed accordingly, in practice, given the challenges inherent in assessing those competencies, most instruction librarians and library instruction programs tend to assess lower-order skills, since they are much easier to quantify. In addition, many of the performance indicators and learning outcomes included in the competency standards are difficult for librarians even to conceive of assessing, since they include competencies that might appear to be more appropriate for faculty to assess, with outcomes such as "participates in classroom discussions" and performance indicators such as "the information literate student communicates the product or performance effectively to others," both of which require a great degree of the type of faculty-librarian collaboration that can be difficult to achieve. The nature of the competency standards allowed librarians mainly to assess lower-order skills-based performance indicators and still maintain that actual assessment had taken place.

While we know that the updated framework for information literacy provides more flexibility, it also challenges librarians to rethink teaching and assessment, moving from skills-based to conceptual instruction. However, authentic teaching, learning, and assessment have the potential to bridge the gaps between the older competencies and the updated frames, moving from skills-based performance indicators to authentic knowledge practices, and to address the higher-order abilities called for in the competency standards. In addition to addressing those higher-order abilities, the updated framework also makes it possible for librarians to address crucial information literacy concepts both inside and outside the library, such as the increasingly important need for social media literacy. In 2017, "two-thirds (67%) of Americans" reported "that they get at least some of their news on social media" (Shearer and Gottfried 2017), which represents a major shift not only in the consumption of news but of information in general over the past few years. The rise of social media presents unique challenges for evaluating authority and credibility, since students are often apt to consult their peers for help in finding and evaluating information before they consult a librarian. In addition, their peers are likely to be connected to them on social media, which might lend information shared on those platforms a patina of authority that it does not warrant. Librarians can use the framework to address these evaluative issues no matter where students encounter information, and authentic teaching and assessment can encourage students to reflect on their own practices and help librarians understand what students are learning. This gap between what students think they know about information and what it actually means to be informary literate is a space that academic librarians can and should address and on which students can and should be assessed. Authentic assessment has the potential to fill those gaps, allowing librarians to perform a necessary service for our students as well as to demonstrate the library's value to the academic institution it serves. Authentic assessment not only makes it possible to better measure students' ability to synthesize and apply what they are learning, but it can also be used to improve librarians' teaching and validate the library's commitment to student success and its centrality to the academic mission. This type of commitment can also help reinforce the academic institution's value to the community that it serves, demonstrating engagement with the kinds of real-world problem-solving skills necessary not only to the twenty-first-century workforce but also to a twenty-first-century citizen's ability to be a successful lifelong learner.

In the end, authentic assessment represents an important shift away from a focus on measuring the bits and pieces that students may have picked up during an individual class to integrating teaching and assessment into one seamless whole. The assessment instrument becomes a tool for both teaching and learning that can be adapted across institutional settings and instructional contexts. Authentic assessments can be formative or summative or include aspects of both. They can be implemented within large first-year information literacy programs or as part of library instruction within upper-level discipline-specific courses. They can be administered as paper-based worksheets, as online documents, or as quizzes embedded in asynchronous online tutorials. Each instrument has its own advantages and challenges, but as outlined in prior chapters authentic assessment is available to any librarian within any context, and it is only a matter of choosing the instrument best suited to an individual's teaching style or instructional context. Authentic teaching, learning, and assessment are only limited by what librarians think they cannot do, not by what they *can* do. And given authentic assessment's capacity to assess student learning and demonstrate library value, this method has the potential to overcome the barriers that librarians often encounter in establishing themselves as respected academic professionals and vital campus partners.

REFERENCES

Association of College and Research Libraries (ACRL). 2000. "Information Literacy Competency Standards for Higher Education." American Library Association, January 18. http://www.ala.org/acrl/sites/ala.org.acrl/files/content/standards/standards.pdf.

Association of College and Research Libraries (ACRL). 2015. "Framework for Information Literacy for Higher Education." American Library Association, February 9. http://www.ala.org/acrl/standards/ilframework.

Shearer, Elisa, and Jeffrey Gottfried. 2017. "News Use across Social Media Platforms 2017." Pew Research Center, September 7. http://www.journalism.org/2017/09/07/news-use-across-social-media-platforms-2017/.

Index

About the Author

Jennifer S. Ferguson is the team lead, arts and humanities, at the Tisch Library of Tufts University, providing innovative and proactive library service in the areas of research, teaching, and learning to undergraduates, graduate students, and faculty. Jennifer has published on topics that include education for librarianship, discovery layer usability, and streaming video in academic libraries, and won the Association of College and Research Libraries–New England Chapter 2017 Best Paper Award. She has also been invited to speak at regional, national, and international conferences on a wide array of topics, including information literacy and authentic assessment. She has a BA from UCLA, an MA from Rutgers University, and an MSLIS from Simmons College, and she has worked in both special and academic libraries.